Footsteps on the Diamond Path

Footsteps on the Diamond Path

Crystal Mirror Series

Volumes I–III (revised and expanded)

Library of Congress Control Number 92021924
LC Call Number BQ7662.2 .F66 1992

ISBN 978-0-89800-243-0

Series editor: Tarthang Tulku. Revisions by Dharma Publishing staff.

Frontispiece: Buddha Gautama and Scenes from his Life. Opaque water-color on canvas, Tibet, 18th century, 39¾ x 23". Reproduced by permission of the Brooklyn Museum 69.164.1. Gift of Mr. and Mrs. Arthur Wiesenberger.

Photographs: Back cover, Lhagang, Tagong in Kham Tibet, courtesy of John Klein. Image of Padmasambhava at bSam-yas monastery blessed by Guru Rinpoche himself, p. 2. The Nyingma Institute in Berkeley, California p.176.

Typeset in Adobe New Aster with New Aster Outline titles and initials. Printed and PUR bound by Dharma Press, 35788 Hauser Bridge Rd., Cazadero, California 95421.

9 8 7 6 5 4 3

Contents

Preface

Many of the articles in this volume were first published
in the early 1970s in volumes I–III of *Crystal Mirror*.
These early volumes of *Crystal Mirror* are no longer in print,
and it seemed valuable to make most of the articles available
in a single new volume, although in a different order. It has
also seemed worthwhile to include some short works
adapted from the Tibetan that originally appeared in *Gesar
Magazine*. If we were redoing these adaptations today, we
would certainly make changes, paying more attention to precise terminology. Still, many people have found these short
selections helpful, and this seems a good opportunity to make
them more readily available.

Several articles retain the informal tone of the early *Crystal Mirrors*. In preparing the articles for publication, the staff
of Dharma Publishing has done some editing, largely for
consistency, but also because over the years we have learned
something about how to present these materials, and we

wanted to pass on the benefit of that knowledge to our readers. In some cases, a more complete or even more accurate
treatment of the same subject can be found in later volumes
of the *Crystal Mirror* Series, but it has still seemed useful to
include a particular selection here, removing errors where
we were aware of them. In the case of some articles by
Tarthang Tulku, we sought and received permission to make
fairly substantial changes, partly to fit the new organization
of the book, and partly to clarify the meaning.

The book is organized around the themes of lineage,
teachings from the tradition, and teachings for the West and
includes a few adaptations from works by great rNying-ma
masters. There is some thematic overlap from one section to
another, which seems unavoidable in a volume like this; perhaps such overlap may allow the reader to see similar
themes in different lights and help to generate new perspec-
tives. In Part Three, Teachings for the West, all articles are
by Tarthang Tulku unless otherwise indicated.

It has been a great joy to work on these selections. In the
essays where the presentation has been substantially shifted,
the teachings themselves have seemed to guide the reshap-
ing, their tremendous value shining through the vocabulary
and syntax. In one sense, reading and rereading these essays
is like discovering in a small way the timelessness of the
Dharma; in another it is like recovering hidden treasures.
We hope that our readers—whether they are long familiar
with Dharma Publishing books or are discovering them for
the first time—will also respond with joy to these selections
and will find them beneficial for both study and practice.

Foreword

Tarthang Tulku

Tibet, my homeland, was a beautiful country—not only because of the natural beauty of its land, but also because of the emphasis on a simple, meaningful way of life. The atmosphere was very supportive of people who wished to devote their time to spiritual practice.

America is also a beautiful land, but this particular quality of support is not so clearly a part of the American tradition. Still, in the face of widespread disillusionment and discontent, more Americans are turning to ancient religions and spiritual disciplines of the East for remedies or alternatives. Vajrayāna Buddhism has always proved extraordinarily powerful in dealing with the problems of human suffering, and it seems this is just as true in the West today as it was for centuries in Tibet.

Buddhism has many levels of teaching, which each individual can understand in accord with his or her own level of mental development. The teachings of the Vajrayāna, which include the teachings of the rNying-ma school, offer a unique method for shortening the way to enlightenment. All that would normally be shunned or overlooked, such as strong emotions, desires, or confusions, are seen as valuable tools. But this path necessarily involves complete openness to each experience, as well as the willingness to investigate thoroughly the causes of dissatisfaction.

As we follow this path, open to whatever arises, there may be times that we become discouraged with our own failings. But this situation too offers the opportunity to learn and to deepen our understanding. To be able to recognize this, we need to encourage one another—our friends and relatives, and whomever we come in contact with—so that each of us can find inspiration in the positive attitude of the Dharma, without too many speculations or confusions.

The use being made of various Eastern systems at present reveals a great deal of indiscriminate mixing of them, an approach that in the long run cannot be very productive. There is also a tendency to accept interpretations that, although optimistic, are very superficial. Isolated from the practice and experience from which they derive, spiritual insights such as "We are all Buddhas" may result only in complacency. Similarly, learned discussions of the nature, virtues, and limitations of a Bodhisattva or advanced yogi can all too easily amount to idle daydreams.

Theory should not be substituted for, or divorced from, first-hand experience. Choosing one discipline and seeing it through to its end is more likely to produce profound results than casually selecting elements from several different traditions. This is why in our publications we attempt to describe the origins and traditions of the Buddhadharma, and more specifically, of the rNying-ma school and the path of Vajrayāna. Our focus on first-hand experience of rNying-ma teachings may also help explain why we have stressed the value of hard work in our practice.

The Buddha's teachings are literally for everyone. They go beyond cultural boundaries and touch the root of each human being's consciousness. The Buddha offered guidance in how to respond wisely to the opportunity offered in each moment to find satisfaction within. The teachings are basically aimed at bringing peace and happiness into our daily lives, both for ourselves and others, and at developing compassion toward all living beings. In practicing the Dharma, we cannot isolate ourselves from the world to the extent that we cannot function well in society. We must learn the way to feel inspiration in all our activities. Knowing that we are traveling a road that eventually will lead to enlightenment, we can appreciate the importance of keeping the Buddhist tradition alive for the benefit of humanity.

I wholeheartedly believe in the effectiveness of the path that rNying-ma offers. For others who may feel that they have found an easier way to achieve enlightenment, I sincerely hope that they do not eventually become disillusioned. Our ordinary mind creates the world of our experience and finds satisfaction in the very tricks and subtleties that cause us suffering. We cannot completely trust this mind.

Although we may have different styles to express ourselves, ultimately we are very much one with all the other people of the world. Each of us is born, each of us will die, and each of us will reap the harvest of his or her past actions. This life will pass like a rainbow in the sky, all too quickly gone—and with it the precious chance to find self-realization. As interest in the Dharma grows, more people feel and understand the impermanence of all samsaric dreams, and the glamors of the material world are seen to shimmer. All this was predicted by the Enlightened One.

May the Gurus of the precious lineage of the Lotus-Born, Padmasambhava, remove all obscurations and hindrances, and may they shower each one of you with love and compassion for all sentient beings.

May the blessings of Buddha and the Lotus-Born Guru nourish those who seek wisdom and truth eternal.

May the lineage of the rNying-ma masters inspire you toward Dharma realization.

May you all be blessed with peace and inspiration in the Dharma, and may whatever merit is acquired by this work be for the benefit and happiness of all humanity.

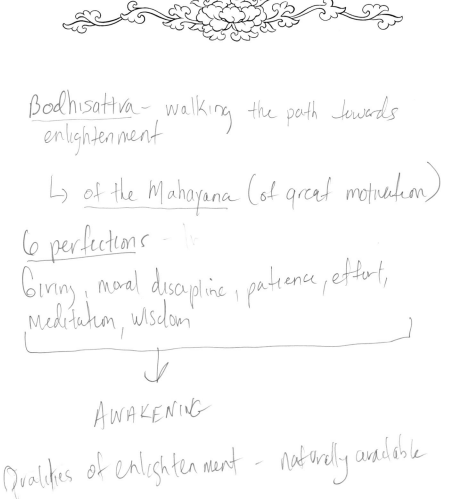

Bodhisattva - walking the path towards enlightenment

↳ of the Mahayana (of great motivation)

6 perfections -

Giving, moral discipline, patience, effort, Meditation, wisdom

↓

AWAKENING

Qualities of enlightenment - naturally available

Introduction

Tarthang Tulku

Buddhism has many different techniques or practices which apply to different situations and to our different levels of consciousness. Some teachings stress self-help through disciplined inquiry and self-control; others emphasize compassion and understanding.

But for all these methods, one principle applies: Just as you cannot talk to a baker about the intricacies of sending a rocket to the moon, so you cannot understand the Dharma properly or deeply without an initial experience of the teachings and a certain amount of practice and skill.

We live in a very scientific, technological society. Modern people are not too interested in religions that stress dogmatic ideas and require rigid conformity. Yet each individual has some basic need for spiritual fulfillment, some deeper, internal source of meaning in life. Here is where the Dharma has special value, for Dharma teachings investigate everything about life and about the world: how we perceive, how we feel, how we judge and think. The path of Dharma is not one of dogma, but of freedom: Through deep meditation and exploration of the mind, awareness develops spontaneously within each situation.

The Buddha's teachings were specifically designed for human consciousness. The tradition founded by the Buddha, as passed on from teacher to student, is very rare and precious—we say 'jewel-like'—precisely because it has proved effective in cutting through the intricacies and subtleties of samsaric mind. But how can we share in this tradition? How can we discover its value in our practice and our lives?

One answer is to make a commitment to exploration. This exploration must take place at a very deep level. For instance, we may search here and search there, but who is doing the searching? We may engage in one or another meditative practice, but what is the actual experience of meditation? How do we look into the thought that accompanies or constitutes an experience? Can we find the 'I' in the events that unfold in the course of each day?

In the Vajrayāna, this questioning takes on a characteristic flavor, because the way of the Vajrayāna is to look behind ideas, conceptions, and pleasures, using each new situation for growth. In Vajrayāna, everything depends on our experience of the teachings in daily life. By questioning this experience, we cut the root of habitual concepts and reactions. As imagined limitations slowly loosen, our energies become liberated from time-consuming confusions and unclear assumptions. Freed from the power of self-grasping concepts, awareness becomes positive, open, and balanced.

In America, there is openness toward a path like this, which encompasses the whole range of experience, for in this land many different kinds of experience are possible. But this very openness can be dangerous, for it is possible to confuse the search for meaning with our continuing efforts to satisfy our needs for pleasure. Since human nature exists in samsara and is governed by samsara, what we feel is most desirable or valuable can often be just another trap. The attitude of 'experimentation' that is so popular here can be very useful, but only if we understand that the material with which we are working, the data we are collecting, is really our own mind. Since this is so, the mind itself, and the self-image that it supports, must also be open to question.

It is just this kind of questioning that the Vajrayāna teachings put at the center of inquiry and practice. Because it works directly with mind at every level, the Vajrayāna can respond to the openness that is so highly developed in America and the West, and at the same time can lead it deeper and expand the vision that guides it.

Because it involves complete openness to each experience, Vajrayāna has always been taught and understood as a path for the very strong. How can we develop this strength, and how can we bring it to our study of the Dharma? Basically, we prepare ourselves to practice Vajrayana by following the tradition of the lineage of teachers who have passed on their wisdom and skillful means from teacher to student since the time of the Buddha.

If we are serious about following in this lineage, we must know its roots, and must make them a part of ourselves. Otherwise, the foundation of our practice will be weak, and whatever we erect will collapse. Knowing the roots means knowing the history of this tradition, for in this way we give firm support to our own inquiry. At the same time, we develop respect, gratitude, and appreciation for past masters of the tradition and what they have done for the sake of the Dharma and the benefit of all beings.

In addition to developing this knowledge, we must be ready to apply the teachings in our own lives. Studying the

Dharma is very different from studying at the university: Success will come only if we allow the teachings to go to the heart of how we live. It is said that how we study the Dharma is actually more important than what we study. The tradition reminds us that to be able to receive teachings is a rare and priceless opportunity. If this is our attitude, we can be confident that success in our study will come.

When we first make contact with the teachings, we may just skim the surface of what is said and grow excited about having discovered something so rich and meaningful, so stimulating and alive. But this is not a solid basis for study. The fruit of the Buddha's teachings comes when we let the Dharma into our lives. Then it truly transforms us, so that in many senses we become a wholly new person.

This transformation comes about only if we are willing to study in a way that involves our whole being. The Dharma is no game; we can gain nothing if we only play at it. When we are able to give ourselves to the guru and to our practices, deep, positive change will come. We must expect to meet obstacles, for much is at stake, but perseverance and patience can counteract these obstacles, and faith can renew our efforts until success is gained.

So to study the Dharma we need to look deeply at our own lives. If we remember and reflect on our past experiences, cultivate awareness in the present, examine the pervasive nature of impermanence, and stay alert to the consequences of our conduct, transformation is possible.

Our problems are mostly self-created. Caught by its concerns, mind runs here and there like a monkey trapped in a house. This situation, with its anxiety and dissatisfaction, can give us the energy to change, to transmute negative mental attitudes. We can learn to use each situation—just as it is—and in this way we can keep meditation a living experience as well. Then we can develop understanding and awareness that stay with us no matter where we are.

Finally, to train ourselves for study of the Vajrayāna we must establish a firm relationship of trust between teacher and student. This is perhaps the most difficult point of all, for here in the West there is no real tradition that could serve as a model for such a relationship. For most students, the relationship they have to their teacher is more external, like a business contract: The student gives effort and various forms of support and expects benefits in return. Tibetans liken the student with this attitude to the musk hunter, who stalks the musk deer for its precious scent, caring nothing for the life of the deer.

In the Vajrayāna, one's guru is held to be even more important than the Buddha, for it is the guru who initiates the student into the teachings. This is fundamental: Without a relationship to a teacher, whatever form this may take, one ultimately cannot tread the path of Vajrayana. And without deep respect and devotion to the teacher, one cannot receive the blessings and power which flow from the Buddha through the teacher's lineage to the student. Many texts speak of this circumstance; to give just one example, the songs of the great yogi Milarepa reflect again and again his gratitude and devotion to Mar-pa for graciously bestowing the gift of his teachings.

Throughout the lineage of Dharma transmission a mutual commitment between teacher and disciple is renewed. Together, they take responsibility to persevere in the practice of the Dharma until full understanding and compassion are born. The key to establishing this relationship is openness and freedom from preconceptions; the key to maintaining it is perseverance in practice and faith in the effectiveness of Buddha and Dharma. It is this dedication to teacher, path, and goal that assures us success as we turn with our hearts, our minds, and our very being to the study of the Dharma.

Footsteps on the Diamond Path

Part One

Lineage

The Life of Śākyamuni Buddha

Although I have shown you the means of liberation, you must know that it depends on you alone.

Śākyamuni

Almost three thousand years ago (according to the reckoning of the most renowned rNying-ma scholar to have considered the issue), the Bodhisattva Śvetaketu, who was to become the Tathāgata Śākyamuni in his next birth, was preaching the Dharma to the devas in Tuṣita Heaven. After absorbing himself in contemplation he looked out through the three-thousand great-thousand world systems and realized that it was time for him to take final rebirth on the continent of Jambudvīpa, in the land of India.

The Birth of the Buddha

In the city of Kapilavastu in northern India (now Nepal), there reigned a great noble Mahārāja, named Śuddhodana. His kingdom was prosperous, his people were happy and

without want, and the Mahārāja was blessed with two fair and faithful wives, the two sisters Māyā and Prajāpatī. But despite the wealth and peace of his kingdom, the Mahārāja was not satisfied, for he had no heir.

Then one night, the Mahārāṇī Māyā dreamt that a great white elephant, with six tusks of the purest ivory, touched her on the right side with his trunk while she lay in a garden dressed in royal robes. When he touched her side, he seemed to melt and pass into her womb. When she awoke, the room was glowing with an orange light, and the music of unseen celestial musicians filled the air.

At lower right in the blockprint on page 5, the Mahārāṇī is seen dreaming in her palace, and at top right the great white elephant is seen attended by devas.*

Śuddhodana rejoiced at the dream and called his seers, who delivered the following interpretation and prophecy: "A Lord of Men is to be born, but whether he will be a temporal or spiritual ruler is uncertain. If, when he is able to judge, he beholds a sick man, an old man, a dead man, and a holy monk, then great and wide will be his kingdom, but not of this world. If he does not behold these things, he will be a Universal Ruler, great in riches, power, and glory." Śuddhodana vowed that his son should never see these things, for his great wish for his son was that he become an even greater ruler than himself.

Soon the Mahārāṇī Māyā was heavy with child. After several months, Māyā, accompanied by her sister Prajāpatī,

---

* The first four woodblock prints illustrating this account belong to a design cut in sDe-dge in Khams around 1720. They reflect the influence of Chinese art that began to take hold at this time, with the increasing involvement of the Manchu dynasty in Tibetan political affairs. The last print was drawn by Khams-sprul Rinpoche at bKra-shis Jong in Khams, a 'Brug-pa bKa'-brgyud monastery. The blocks were carved in Thub-bstan-rnam-rgyal dGon-pa.

traveled to the house of her parents—following the custom of her people that the child should be born there. During their journey, they passed the Lumbinī Gardens in what today is southern Nepal, and Māyā commanded the caravan to stop so that she might wander awhile in the cool shade of the trees.

In this garden, standing beneath a great palsa tree, the Mahārāṇī felt the oncoming birth of the child. As she seized a bough of the tree, the Bodhisattva emerged from her right side. His body and speech possessed the thirty-two marks and eighty characteristics of the perfected being, and when he emerged, it seemed to the handmaidens that the sun had just come from behind a cloud.

The newborn child took seven steps, and lotuses sprang up under his feet. Then he declared: "Thus have I come for the well-being of the world. This is my last birth!" In the blockprint (lower left), the infant prince, his right hand in the gesture of fearlessness, is shown before seven lotus blossoms, while above him devas anoint his head with the nectar of immortality. Seven days later, the Mahārāṇī Māyā passed into the heaven realms. At upper left in the blockprint, two devas are shown in Tuṣita Heaven, holding the crown of the Bodhisattva who abandoned it to return to human birth.

The Prince Siddhārtha

The newborn prince received the name Siddhārtha, "He who has attained his aim." When the time came for Siddhārtha's instruction, Śuddhodana summoned the sage Viśvamitra. Yet when Viśvamitra questioned him, there was nothing Siddhārtha did not know. In the blockprint on the following page (upper right), teacher and pupil are shown seated in a small pagoda.

Śuddhodana had received his newborn son with the greatest joy, but now he was uneasy. He resolved that

Siddhārtha must never have the inclination or opportunity to renounce his kingdom. Thus the Mahārāja Śuddhodana built four palaces, one for each season, and took every care that Siddhārtha should always be surrounded by sensual beauty. In the central image of the blockprint, Siddhārtha, attired in princely robes, is seated on a throne with his father at his side, while lovely maidens sing and dance for his amusement.

Despite countless delights and distractions, Prince Siddhārtha would often withdraw from the pleasures of the senses and spend hours in deep meditation. The prince's periods of introspection greatly worried Śuddhodana. So he sent for Yaśodharā, the most beautiful princess of all the surrounding kingdoms. Yaśodharā, a maiden of unblemished character, genuinely pleased the young prince.

In accordance with custom, athletic contests were proclaimed to decide who should have Yaśodharā's hand. Siddhārtha, seemingly abandoning his detached reflections, joined the contests with a will. He showed himself superior in every way.

He is shown at lower right with discharged bow, having just driven an arrow through the trunks of three trees and an iron pig's head. Above the archery scene, Siddhārtha exhibits his skill in swimming, and at bottom left he is shown relaxing, having just tossed an elephant into a river.

Although living in the midst of amusements and enjoyments, Siddhārtha expressed a wish to visit the royal gardens outside the city. One day, Śuddhodana allowed his son to travel through the city by chariot, but only after strict instructions to the townspeople that the sick, old, or dead were not to be seen on Siddhārtha's journey.

But the devas assumed human form to help awaken the prince to his purpose. During the chariot ride, Siddhārtha saw a sick man and an old man (at the right), and finally, the body of a dead man, over which two vultures were hovering (bottom left). Thus were Siddhārtha's eyes opened to the common lot of all incarnate life.

After meeting a holy man, shown at the right with begging bowl and staff, Siddhārtha resolved to renounce his inheritance and search for a way to relieve all beings from suffering incurred by old age, sickness, and death. One night, the attendants assigned to keep watch on the prince fell asleep through the work of the devas. Siddhārtha, seeing his chance, saddled his faithful stallion. Accompanied by a host of devas, who held up the hooves of the horse lest they wake the sleeping palace guards, the young prince left his father's kingdom, fulfilling the prophecy that had attended his birth.

The Great Renunciation

Far from his father's kingdom, Siddhārtha removed his jewels and ornaments and, turning to his servant Chandaka, said, "Take these jewels to my father and tell him that, with no lack of love or feeling of anger, I have entered the woods of the ascetics to destroy old age and death." In the blockprint, Siddhārtha is shown in the act most symbolic of his great renunciation: With his knife he cuts off the knot of hair which as a prince he wore twisted with jewels. Below him, attendant devas catch the hair as it falls.

Then he traded his princely robes with a passing hunter who was attired in coarse red cloth. Above Siddhārtha to the left are shown in their caves the Himalayan ascetics to whom Siddhārtha went for teaching. In the five-mountain Vindhya range Siddhārtha met the Brahmin Alara, who became his first teacher. The young renunciate learned the sacred scriptures and joined in the strong chanting of the Vedic hymns. When he needed food, he went to the city below, begging from house to house (bottom left).

But Siddhārtha soon found that the singing of Vedic hymns and the learning of ancient scriptures did not convey the knowledge that eased the existential sorrow of beings. He then went to the famed teachers Ārāḍa Kālāma and Udraka Rāmaputra but was not satisfied. Both clung to the concept of a soul, and in this the Bodhisattva perceived the seed of suffering.

Having exhausted the wisdom of the greatest teachers, Siddhārtha resolved to go into the forest to practice the path of asceticism. He journeyed to the banks of the river Nairañjanā, where, in company with five ascetics who had followed him, he began his austerities. He practiced staring like a deer until he could gaze into the horizon for days without count, forgetting the body and its pain, forgetting the mind and its wandering. Eating almost nothing, he renounced the desires of the body, going ever deeper into meditation. This he did for six long years, until his body withered to skin and bones. When he desired food, he would beg single grains of rice or single jujube fruits, and in this way he warded off death.

Finally, secure in the knowledge that this path also was limited, Siddhārtha, now known as Śākyamuni, the Sage of the Śākyas, abandoned the way of mortification and resolved to restore his body to health. On his way out of the forest, he received some milk and accepted an armful of pure and pliant kuśa grass from a farmer (p.11, lower right). Then he made his way to Bodh Gayā. Spreading the grass beneath the Bodhi Tree, he seated himself with folded hands and feet, with the resolve to win complete enlightenment.

The Final Enlightenment

As the Bodhisattva sat beneath the Bodhi Tree, steadfast in his resolve to win perfect insight, Māra, King of Desire, who brings delight to the senses and clouds the intellect, came with his demon hordes. Failing to frighten the Bodhisattva

from his purpose, Māra asked by what virtue he could claim the right to enlightenment. With his right hand the Bodhisattva touched the ground beneath the Bodhi Tree and called the Earth to witness his countless lifetimes dedicated to liberating beings from all sources of sorrow. Acknowledging his claim, the Earth shook in six ways.

Prepared to do battle, Māra shot an arrow at the Bodhisattva and sent his daughters Lust, Delight, and Craving with his sons Confusion, Gaiety, and Pride to disturb Siddhārtha's calmness of mind. Many apparitions now appeared before the Bodhisattva. His wife, Yaśodharā (shown directly beneath the Buddha), appeared and knelt at his feet. Māra's daughters, appearing in the form of beautiful young maidens, begged him to abandon his life of detachment and return to the pleasures of his kingdom. But nothing swayed the Bodhisattva. Through his power, Māra's lovely daughters became transformed into ugly hags even as they spoke.

Then Māra, bitterly afraid and ashamed of defeat, ordered his army to attack the Bodhisattva with spears of copper, flaming swords, and caldrons of boiling oil. They came riding decaying corpses and lashing out with hooks and whips and spiked wheels of fire. Some sprouted flames from every hair or rode mad elephants through the tree tops. The earth shook, and the regions of space flashed flames. Yet whenever any implement of barbed or flaming destruction came near the Bodhisattva, it turned into a rain of flowers, fragrant and gentle to the touch. Then the voice of a celestial being addressed Māra, saying, "O Māra, cease this vain fatigue. Throw aside enmity and retreat to peace. This Sage will no more be shaken by you than Mt. Meru by a fickle wind." Māra, beaten, ceased his torment, and the Sage's mind was still.

It was the first watch, and the Bodhisattva, his consciousness opening to infinity, perceived a continuous vision of all his past lives and rebirths. In the second watch, he beheld all that lives and the transient round of birth and death of all humanity.

In the third watch, there came still broader vision, in which he beheld the causes of the chain of existence and how all suffering proceeds from ignorance. Having thus perceived the world as it is, Śākyamuni, shorn of all vestiges of illusion, attained Anuttara-samyak-sambodhi, complete, perfect enlightenment. From that moment he became the Bhagavan, the Sugata, the Tathāgata—the perfectly enlightened Buddha.

Turning the Wheel of the Dharma

After the Buddha attained complete enlightenment, he considered whether or not to teach the Dharma, for he thought no one would understand the depth of his experience. But Brahmā, knowing the Sage's thought, left the highest heavens and appeared before the Buddha, saying, "Please do not pass into the forest like a rhinoceros and adopt the habit of a recluse. All the Sugatas of the past have fulfilled their vow and have turned the Wheel of the Immaculate Dharma. Do as they have done, for the benefit of living beings."

The Tathāgata assented and thought that it would be best to present his realization first to his five former ascetic companions. As the Buddha approached Sārnāth, the five mendicants saw him coming and said to one another, "There is Gautama, who has abandoned the ascetic path for the luxuries of the world. Let us not rise to greet him, nor pay homage, nor offer him a seat." But when the Buddha approached, so powerful was his vow and so calm was his mind that against their will they immediately rose and offered him the highest seat. One took his robe and one washed his feet while the others made respectful greetings. Then the Buddha said, "Do not address me as Gautama any longer, for I am the Buddha, and by my own effort I have attained what is difficult to attain."

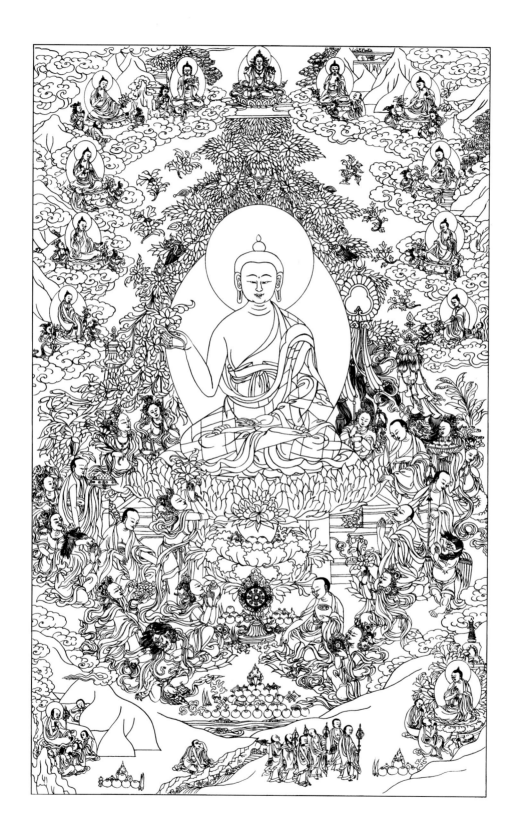

Then he began turning the Wheel of the Dharma, teaching each according to his capabilities. For those of lesser understanding, he taught that samsara is a burning house and that the discipline of a monk is the proper method to escape the Wheel of Birth and Death. For those of more developed consciousness, he conveyed the profound emptiness that characterizes all reality and taught that a compassionate intention towards all beings will liberate the whole of samsara. And to those most advanced, he taught the method of realizing non-dual insight and obtaining enlightenment in a single lifetime. Three times he turned the Wheel of the Dharma in all, bringing the teaching into all the six realms of existence. Gathering around him the disciples and Bodhisattvas, he revealed the path that leads to liberation from sorrow and opens the gateway to nirvana for the welfare of all beings. In the course of time he founded the Sangha, so that the Dharma might be preserved, and future generations might be guided by the living example of those who follow the Buddha's teachings.

In the blockprint, the Tathāgata is shown on the Vulture Peak at Rājagṛha, preaching the Sūtra known as the Lotus of the True Law, a Mahāyāna text. With disciples in attendance, making offerings and requesting teachings, the Enlightened One illuminates the entire universe, from the highest heavens to the lowest hell realms, with a ray of light that springs from his eyebrows, reaching into other universes governed by a different space and time, where countless other Buddhas are simultaneously teaching the Lotus Sūtra.

Three Paths
to Liberation

The Buddha's teaching is called forth by the different needs and varying capacities of living beings.

Thousands of years ago the Buddha first turned the Wheel of the Dharma at the Deer Park near Vārāṇasī. Like the blazing sun, it revolved across the heavens, and its sound still reverberates down through the ages.

Because human beings are of varying dispositions and different levels of spiritual development, the Buddha, out of his infinite compassion, taught the Dharma according to the intellectual development and comprehension of each disciple. Thus there come down to us various traditions of what the Buddha taught.

To some the Buddha proclaimed the Hīnayāna and the perfection of the Arhat. To others, able to comprehend the meaning of śūnyatā and aspire to Buddha-like perfection, he expounded the royal road of the Mahāyāna. To those disciples able to benefit from a direct path to enlightenment, he revealed the Vajrayāna or Diamond Way.

The Hīnayāna and Mahāyāna are based directly on the Sūtras, while the Vajrayāna is based not only on the Sūtras but on the Tantras as well. The Sūtras were written down centuries after the time of the Buddha; the Tantras were handed down through a secret oral tradition from master to disciple for a thousand years before being committed to writing. It is thus that the written texts of the Tantras appear much later than those of the Sūtras.

Those who enter upon the Hīnayāna or Narrow Path seek the perfection of the Arhat. One meaning of the term Arhat is 'he who has the slain the enemies'; that is, the kleśas or defilements. The kleśas are the outer layer of obscurations and confusions interfering with mental clarity; they consist of all one's negative emotions and selfish impulses. The Arhat counters the kleśas by attaining realization of anatman, the unreality and non-substantiality of the ego or self concept (atma-śūnyatā). By means of strenuous renunciation and ascetic discipline, practiced through innumerable lives, the disciple succeeds in cutting off and utterly annihilating all feeling, emotion, and impulse, attaining the nirvana of the perfect Arhat.

Those who enter the Mahāyāna, the Great Path, are called Bodhisattvas. Motivated by compassion, Bodhisattvas dedicate themselves to the enlightenment of all beings. Their training requires countless lives of intense striving, based on the deliberate effort to nurture, cultivate, and mature the six perfections of giving, moral conduct, patience, vigor, meditation, and wisdom. Through the perfection of wisdom the Bodhisattva attains realization of the unreality of all dharmas (constituents of phenomenal existence). This is dharmaśūnyatā, and its realization removes the deeper layer of obscurations covering the mind, consisting of mistaken views and metaphysical fictions.

At the outset of spiritual training, the Bodhisattva undertakes the great vow of the Bodhisattva: to strive with all his will and effort for enlightenment but to postpone final attainment of nirvana in order to aid, comfort, and rescue all sentient beings who still remain entrapped in the bondage of samsara. Thus the Bodhisattva equally embraces compassionate meritorious activity and perfect insight.

While the Mahāyāna path of the Bodhisattva requires innumerable lives for the attainment of liberation, those who enter the Diamond Path of the Vajrayāna may attain enlightenment in this very life and in this very body. The Vajrayāna is part of the Mahāyāna, but is the short path directly up the steep face of the mountain. For this reason, it requires guidance from an accomplished master. The Tantras and secret mantras of the Vajrayāna are given only to the initiated, for left to themselves, individuals who lack spiritual maturity will only misconstrue the teachings, or even worse, abuse them for selfish purposes.

The interplay of Hīnayāna, Mahāyāna, and Vajrayāna is a complicated topic, and there are many other ways of characterizing the different yānas that the Buddha presented. The word yāna literally means vehicle, and it is said that different vehicles are appropriate for different individuals. Thus the Mahāyāna most often distinguishes three yānas. The first two, the Śrāvakayāna and Pratyekabuddhayāna, are generally linked to the Hīnayāna. They are distinguished from each other by the nature of the insight that their followers attain. The third is the Bodhisattvayāna, and corresponds to the path followed in the Mahāyāna tradition.

In the rNying-ma teachings, six additional yānas are recognized, each based on a different aspect of the teachings of the Tantras. In this way, the rNying-ma school recognizes nine yānas in all, each contributing to the universality of the Buddha's teachings.

Guru Padmasambhava

I shall come to this world for the sake of its people.

Guru Padmasambhava, the Lotus-Born Teacher, is the great master of the Vajrayāna who brought Buddhism to Tibet in the eighth century C.E. The rNying-ma-pa, the most ancient of the four major schools of Tibetan Buddhism, preserves the teachings introduced and expounded by Padmasambhava and the sage Śāntarakṣita. Deeply revered by all Tibetan Buddhists and regarded as a second Buddha, Padmasambhava is responsible for the preservation and transmission of Vajrayāna Buddhism in Tibet.

One of the biographies of Padmasambhava, written by his disciple, the Tibetan princess Ye-shes-mtsho-rgyal, recounts the Precious Guru's birth, his experiences as a young prince, his subsequent renunciation of worldly life and his search for esoteric teachings. This is the 'ordinary' man, who studies all aspects of the Dharma under the guidance of the great gurus and scholars of the time (including Ānanda, the

Buddha's cousin). It is this man who seems to attain perfection through deep meditation, and then through his perfect realization of Truth, manifests himself in various forms and performs miracles to teach the Dharma, the Great Liberation, to all sentient beings.

Ye-shes-mtsho-rgyal's biography clearly indicates that the Vajra Guru transcends ordinary reality. Padmasambhava embodies the essence of the Buddhas of the Three Times, the three kāyas, and the ten directions. Certain Buddhas have specific powers for particular purposes. Padmasambhava's specially empowered essence is uniquely manifested for all sentient beings through a variety of forms which he assumes at various times to teach the esoteric doctrines. All these forms, whether as a deity in a wrathful or peaceful aspect or in some other form entirely, are created out of his "Truth-Form" to aid all beings in the attainment of enlightenment.

Even though to our samsaric eyes the actions or behavior of Padmasambhava may seem to conform to the ordinary human way, this is done only to enable us to have confidence and to follow the True Path, to lead us out of blinding ignorance and doubt. From the time of his miraculous birth, prophesied by the Buddha, he is the perfectly Enlightened One. But we need to see the ordinary ways, or we cannot understand, we cannot believe, and so we will not follow.

Padmasambhava's incarnation is specifically suited for the Kāli Yuga. Carefully preserved, revealed, and transmitted through the Tibetan tradition, the full power, the pure, unadulterated essence of the original or primordial teachings are released to all who pray to him and follow the path to enlightenment. This is not mythology, a fairy tale, or speculation; and certainly it is not limited to a simple, story-like form. Like similar yogic texts, the life story of Padmasambhava is written in highly symbolic language, expressions of the experiences of meditation through events in the outer world. Buddhists meet the questions of the validity or actuality of Padmasambhava's miracles in terms of the symbolic and magical nature of reality, or of the mind itself. To reflect on this, consider that five hundred years ago flying was a miracle; today it is commonplace.

Padmasambhava is not intended to be viewed solely as an historical person. His bodily form is like a pure reflection, the visible appearance of the mind and compassion of all Buddhas. Padmasambhava and the Buddha are identical. He is all the Buddhas, past, present, and future—timeless, beyond birth and death.

We can experience this same primordial Buddha nature within ourselves. In Vajrayāna Buddhism, Padmasambhava is neither a deity nor a mythological figure—he is the gateway through which the powers and divine qualities of the Buddha can be received, the focal point of practices that lead the aspirant to liberation. Constant and mindful meditation on the pure essence of the Guru purifies body, speech, and mind, transforming ordinary consciousness into the highest wisdom and transcending ordinary forms. Vajrayāna teaches that transformation can be accomplished in this very lifetime.

This sādhana, or spiritual practice, of Padmasambhava is especially important and effective in times plagued by excessive materialism and strong desires, such as the present age. By practicing his teachings, we can benefit ourselves and others. It is the Precious Guru's promise:

"I shall come every morning and every evening to the abode of those who have faith in me. I shall come to this world for the sake of its people."

The drawings which follow are the nine manifestations of the Guru from wood blocks cut in sDe-dge, in eastern Tibet.

Guru Padma 'byung-gnas

Guru Śākya Seng-ge

Guru U-rgyan rDo-rje-'chang

Guru Padma rgyal-po

Guru Blo-ldan-mchog-sred

Guru Padmasambhava

Guru Nyi-ma-'od-zer

Guru rDo-rje-gro-lod

Guru Seng-ge-sgra-sgrogs

The Development
of Tibetan Buddhism

*Tibet was the perfect receptacle for the unfolding of
the Vajrayāna.*

Tibet was destined by its circumstances to become one of
the greatest Buddhist cultures ever to unfold. The high
elevation of the Himalayas created an atmosphere of calm
and quiet. Within the isolation enforced by nature, the mind
tended naturally to be peaceful, able to concentrate and
think clearly, without distraction or disturbance. Blessed
with such fortunate conditions for the practice of meditation, Tibet was the perfect receptacle for the unfolding of the
Vajrayāna, the last major vehicle presented by the Buddha
for the sake of leading all beings to enlightenment.

Yet at the time of the Buddha Śākyamuni, Tibet was a
sparsely populated and undeveloped expanse, ringed by
snow-covered mountains. Very gradually a civilization began
to form. A lineage of kings was established to act as leaders

for the people. Eventually, in the seventh century C.E., Tibet ascended to a place of prominence among the powers of Asia.

When Srong-btsan-sgam-po, the thirty-second Tibetan king, assumed the throne late in the sixth century or early in the seventh, his country exerted considerable influence in many parts of Asia. Buddhism thrived in numerous lands, and Tibet's expansion into its neighboring countries provided a natural exposure to the Buddhist tradition and culture. As an incarnation of Avalokiteśvara, the Bodhisattva of Boundless Compassion, Srong-btsan-sgam-po was well-empowered to introduce and provide the foundation for Buddhism in Tibet. He knew the importance of a firm basis in moral discipline and formulated ten moral principles and sixteen rules of public conduct for his people. These closely resembled the fundamental precepts of conduct and practice established by the Buddha centuries earlier.

Srong-btsan-sgam-po recognized the value of strong ties with countries where Buddhism was already established. To facilitate close relations with China and Nepal, he married a Chinese and a Nepalese princess, incarnations of Green Tārā and White Tārā. Each princess brought a sacred image of the Buddha with her to Tibet. These greatly treasured statues, made with precious metals and gems, possessed the qualities of the Wish-Fulfilling Gem. Their arrival inspired the building of the first Buddhist temples in Tibet.

Some texts of the Buddhist scriptures were also brought to Tibet at this time, but no written form of the Tibetan language yet existed. Consequently, the king sent his minister Thon-mi Sambhoṭa and sixteen others to India to study the language and literature of the Dharma. This was the first of many such journeys that would be made to and from India for the sake of establishing the Dharma. For those who undertook the journey, there were great hardships. If they survived the travel over treacherous terrain and reached India, they had still to endure the great contrast between the climates of Tibet and India. Many Tibetans died en route or during their studies in India.

After many years of intense study, Thon-mi returned to Tibet, the only survivor of the mission. There he composed a script and eight volumes of grammar and orthography suitable for Tibetan, a precise and flexible language. While maintaining a close relationship to spoken Tibetan, the new written language was carefully designed as a vehicle for the teachings. Many new words were created especially for Dharma translations: Preserving the distinction between ordinary and higher levels, these new terms had great power. All these characteristics enhance the precision and purity of Tibetan translations of Buddhist texts.

Srong-btsan-sgam-po taught a few select students the ways of Avalokiteśvara. He built one hundred and eight temples and over one thousand stūpas. Despite his efforts, however, Buddhism remained largely confined to central Tibet in the region around lHa-sa. This was the result of frequent and numerous hindrances, including the dominance of the Bon tradition. Associated with the ancient shamanistic practices and with sorcery, Bon was a significant obstruction to the spread of Buddhism.

Not until several generations later, under King Khri-srong-lde-btsan, did Buddhism spread throughout Tibet. Khri-srong-lde-btsan's efforts were also met with many disruptions, and under his rule the strength of the Bon opposition became manifest. But the king, an incarnation of Mañjuśrī, the Lord of Limitless Wisdom, persisted. He succeeded in bringing many noted paṇḍitas to Tibet from India, including the Mahāpaṇḍita Śāntarakṣita, the great Guru Padmasambhava, and the tantric master Vimalamitra.

Śāntarakṣita was the first of these great masters to arrive. When his efforts to spread the Dharma were successfully countered by the various forces opposing Buddhism, he advised the king to send for Padmasambhava, the supreme siddha renowned for his incomparable scholarship and psychic power. Knowing that his country needed this enlightened master to kindle the flame of the Dharma, Khri-srong-lde-btsan immediately dispatched messengers laden with gold as offerings to the Vajra Guru.

Padmasambhava is considered the manifestation of the Buddhas of past, present, and future. Famed throughout the Three Realms—the Desire Realm in which we live, and the Realms of Form and Formlessness—he was fully aware in advance of the mission of the Tibetan emissaries, and met them in the region now known as Nepal. He knew he would journey with these couriers back to Tibet, conquer the interfering powers, and plant the seed of the Vajrayāna. But before revealing himself as the one they sought, he questioned the messengers as if to ascertain their purpose.

When offered the gold sent by the king, Padmasambhava flung it in the ten directions as offerings to the Dharma. The messengers were greatly alarmed by this gesture, and doubted the wisdom of this man who so casually threw away their country's fortune. Aware of their concern, Padmasambhava bade them hold out their robes, and when they did so, he miraculously filled them with gold.

The Lotus-Born Master cut through the demonic and negative forces interrupting the progress of Buddhism in Tibet and converted them to the way of the Dharma. Some were made Dharma protectors, some were given vows, others were ensured the chance to obtain enlightenment. Through Padmasambhava's efforts it became possible to build bSam-yas monastery as a center for study of the Dharma. When he blessed the images and pictures inside the temple at bSam-yas, they came alive. In this way converting darkness to light, Padmasambhava cleared the way for the development of Vajrayāna.

bSam-yas Monastery

Padmasambhava had twenty-five great disciples, each a supreme siddha renowned for a particular psychic power. Among them were Ye-shes-mtsho-rgyal (the embodiment of learning), King Khri-srong-lde-btsan, and Vairotsana. Guru Padmasambhava taught his disciples the nature of the Kāli Yuga and the kinds of instructions and practices to give at particular times, making many accurate predictions about the coming ages and teaching the means of initiations for all instructions. Some of his teachings were hidden. Padmasambhava continues to be available to people today, assuming many manifestations to help those of this dark age.

Through the patronage of Khri-srong-lde-btsan and the spiritual guidance of Guru Padmasambhava, Śāntarakṣita, Vimalamitra, and others, the Dharma developed rapidly. Many of the texts presenting the major philosophical views and ethical practices were translated under the guidance of Śāntarakṣita, whose lineage included the teachings of the two major philosophical schools, Mādhyamika and Yogācāra. At the same time, Padmasambhava, Vimalamitra, and many others taught the higher esoteric teachings of the Mantrayāna.

In translating the major texts, Tibet's great lo-tsā-bas (translators) worked with the Indian paṇḍitas invited by the king. Before these masters of Dharma and language even attempted to translate the original scriptures into Tibetan, they thoroughly studied Sanskrit and Tibetan, received initiation into the teachings, and mastered the practices. When translation began, each aspect of every text was carefully discussed to ensure the purity of the transmission. Today, when many of the original manuscripts for these texts are no longer available, these translations are often invaluable to establish the authentic meaning of a text. They are considered among the most precise translations ever rendered of the Buddha's teachings.

In the early ninth century, the Dharma king Ral-pa-can (ruled 815–836) invited additional paṇḍitas to Tibet. These scholars worked with the Tibetan lo-tsā-bas to standardize the terms used for translating Dharma concepts from Sanskrit. They compiled the first dictionary, which was indispensable for future translations. Ral-pa-can, an incarnation of Vajrapāṇi, also established the first system of public support for the monastic Sangha by decreeing that every seven households were to provide for the needs of one monk.

In 836, Glang Dar-ma, Ral-pa-can's irreligious older brother who had been bypassed for the throne, had his younger brother assassinated. His was a reign of terror that threatened the destruction of the Dharma in Tibet. Fortunately, the Vinaya and Mantrayāna lineages were preserved intact throughout this time. Three monks known as dMar, Rab, and gYo escaped with the Vinaya texts to eastern Tibet where, with the assistance of several Chinese masters, they ordained Bla-chen dGongs-pa rab-gsal. Bla-chen ordained his disciple Klu-mes and nine other men from the central provinces of dBus and gTsang. When hostilities ceased, these ten men returned to the central provinces.

By taking on the role of ordinary laymen, masters entrusted with the transmission of the esoteric teachings managed to preserve them in an unbroken lineage. The teachings preserved in this way are the bKa'-ma, the formalized, practical codification of the Mantrayāna teachings transmitted by Padmasambhava, Vimalamitra, Vairotsana and others, and continued to the present in an unbroken lineage transmitted from master to disciple. To be transmitted properly, these teachings must be given in accord with method, which includes 1) instruction, which is essential to understanding; 2) system or tradition, through which the instruction is given; and 3) experience. These three elements are integrated through sādhana.

Also passed on in the same way were the teachings known as gTer-ma, which were concealed by Padmasambhava to be rediscovered at the intended time. It is difficult to explain exactly what the gTer-ma are, how they are established, and where they are found, due in part to differences between English and Tibetan. gTer are classified into eighteen different categories, based primarily on the subject (the 'what') and where they come from. The Tibetan names for the gTer revelations indicate the qualities that characterize their emergence.

The rediscovery of gTer-ma began as early as the tenth century and flourished especially from the fourteenth through the sixteenth centuries. Under the auspices of the gTer-stons (gTer-ma masters), such rediscoveries continue today. The continuing revelation of Tantra afforded by these hidden treasures is of indisputable value and importance. Their rediscovery by gTer-stons releases an invaluable force at crucial times—times when the light of these teachings is especially needed to cut through the darkness of ignorance.

Although the original lineage of masters and the teachings still maintained its original purity, the persecution of the doctrine under Glang Dar-ma disrupted the development of Buddhism in Tibet. Beginning at the end of the tenth century, Tibetans once again made great sacrifices to travel to India to study with the great masters and obtain their lineages. The lineages brought back to Tibet during this period gave rise to new traditions of practice, which in time became formalized into schools. These schools became known as the new or gSar-ma schools, while those who maintained the lineages brought to Tibet in the early transmission then became known as rNying-ma, the Ancient Ones.

In the tenth and eleventh centuries, great Indian and Tibetan scholars compiled new translations. Among these translators perhaps the foremost was Rin-chen-bzang-po (958–1051), who had studied Sanskrit and Dharma for many years in Kashmir. In 1042, when the great Indian master Atīśa was invited to Tibet by Ye-shes 'Od, the king of Gu-ge, he visited Tho-lding monastery, where Rin-chen-bzang-po was abbot. Atīśa was amazed at Tibet's great treasury of Tantras and commentaries, far more extensive than anything he had ever seen in his travels throughout India.

Atīśa and his disciples worked at Tho-lding to revise the new Tibetan translations, clarifying confusing or elusive points. While there Atīśa also wrote a famous work in Sanskrit known as the Bodhipathāpradīpa, or Lamp That Shows the Path to Enlightenment.

Atīśa was disturbed by reports that Buddhist practices were not being purely maintained in Tibet. To investigate the validity of these claims, he decided to visit the great lama Kun-mkhyen Rong-zom Chos-kyi-bzang-po, one of the most famous lamas in the rNying-ma lineage. Rong-zom, a great scholar and lo-tsā-ba, was the author of commentaries on the Mahāyoga and Anuyoga Tantras and on several Sūtras that are still among the most important for understanding rNying-ma thought. As soon as they met, Atīśa recognized Rong-zom as the reincarnation of his own guru, Nag-po-pa, and his doubts were dispelled. As for Atīśa himself, in his autobiography he refers to his own previous incarnation as Lama Dri-ma-med-pa'i-dpal, a name for Padmasambhava. Through Atīśa, Padmasambhava continued to give his blessings to all sentient beings.

The teachings of Atīśa led to the founding of the bKa'-gdams-pa school, which offered a very practical approach to the Bodhisattva path. The bKa'-gdams-pa studied and practiced six 'doctrines', including the Bodhicaryāvatāra of Śāntideva, the Sūtras, and monastic rules and ethics. Their approach emphasized a gradual, step-by-step progression.

Mar-pa Lo-tsā-ba, a younger contemporary, prepared other key translations, and his work later formed the basis for the bKa'-brgyud-pa school. A successful scholar who studied for years in India, he translated numerous Tantras. Although he studied with many great masters in India, his root guru was the great siddha Nāropa. On one of his trips to India, Mar-pa met Atīśa, who urged him to return to Tibet with him. However, Mar-pa had been instructed by Nāropa to travel to India three times, so he declined the invitation.

For a school to be truly formed, it must establish monasteries, a lineage, and a particular doctrinal approach. One of Mar-pa's most famed and successful disciples, Milarepa (Mi-la-ras-pa) succeeded in attaining enlightenment through his yogic practices. But it was not until sGam-po-pa, Milarepa's disciple and another incarnation of Padmasambhava, that the monastic system, rules, and ethics of the bKa'-brgyud-pa evolved. sGam-po-pa did a great deal toward clarifying the meditational and practical applications of philosophical concepts characteristic of the bKa'-brgyud-pa approach. Many of the esoteric sādhanas, rituals, and teachings of this school are related to the rNying-ma approach. It is said that the bKa'-brgyud-pa were so successful that the range of their teaching extended in all directions as far as an eagle can fly in eighteen days.

The Sa-skya-pa school formed around another set of translated tantric texts late in the thirteenth century. This sect derived its name from the color of the soil in the area southwest of gShis-ka-rtse where it was formed. Until the time of Kun-dga'-snying-po, the Sa-skya followed the direct lineage of Padmasambhava; under his leadership, however, they shifted their focus to the New Translation tradition.

The Sa-skya have contributed many great lamas to the Dharma. They developed three schools and established two major monasteries. Like all schools of Tibetan Buddhism, the Sa-skya study and practice several key sādhanas preserved in the rNying-ma tradition. The Vajrakīla, a rNying-ma tantra and sādhana continued through the lineage of Padmasambhava, is central in the Sa-skya school. At one time, their influence expanded to the point where they dominated the political rule of Tibet.

Padmasambhava is revered in the Sa-skya tradition, and many of the great Sa-skya lamas were considered reincarnations of Padmasambhava. One such lama was Sa-skya Paṇḍita Kun-dga'-rgyal-mtshan, the grandson of Kun-dga'-snying-po. Sa-skya-Paṇḍita helped reestablish and rebuild bSam-yas monastery. Known for his knowledge of Sanskrit, he transmitted Tibetan Buddhism to Mongolia as well as to parts of China.

The last major school of Tibetan Buddhism to form was founded by Tsong-kha-pa in the fourteenth century. Tsong-kha-pa was a great master who studied and practiced extensively and was a very pure monk. His principal teachers were rJe-btsun Red-mda'-ba, a great Sa-skya master, bKa'-gdams-pa Rol-pa'i-rdo-rje, and the great rNying-ma master Grub-chen Las-kyi-rdo-rje. Honored as an incarnation of Mañjuśrī,

Tsong-kha-pa and his disciples founded the dGe-lugs-pa, the only exclusively celibate school of Tibetan Buddhism.

The dGe-lugs-pa maintain a very high scholastic reputation and emphasize the importance of strict renunciation through the monastic life and the Bodhisattva vow. By the sixteenth century they were very influential, and at the time of the Fifth Dalai Lama (also revered as a great rNying-ma master), the Dalai Lama emerged as the recognized head of the government of Tibet. Viewed as an incarnation of Avalokiteśvara, the Dalai Lama acts on behalf of the Dharma; for several centuries the Paṇ-chen Lama, considered an incarnation of the Buddha Amitābha (Buddha of Infinite Light), has played a similar role. The present ruler, His Holiness the Fourteenth Dalai Lama, continues to act as the leader of the Tibetan people, even though in exile in India. Through his wisdom and guidance, it is hoped that the precious teachings of Tibetan Buddhism may continue the spread of the Buddhadharma.

The rNying-ma tradition still continues today, its teachings empowered through the unbroken original lineage. Many rNying-ma teachings are preserved in the bKa'-'gyur, which contains one hundred and eight volumes of the Buddha's teachings, and the bsTan-'gyur, comprising two hundred fifty volumes of commentary.

However, the highest tantric teachings of the rNying-ma school, the inner Tantras of the Mahā-, Anu-, and Atiyoga, are found primarily in the compilation known as the rNying-ma rGyud-'bum (One Hundred Thousand Nyingma Tantras) and in the sixty-three volumes of the Rin-chen-gter-mdzod, which contains key texts rediscovered by the one hundred and eight great gTer-ma masters predicted by Padmasambhava. All these works have been the subject of extensive scholarship and have occasioned countless commentaries concerned with the inner meaning and direct application of the teachings.

Although neither materially wealthy nor politically active, the rNying-mas have many accomplished yogis and masters. When problems or disasters have arisen in the course of Tibetan history, it has often been the rNying-ma-pa, whose resources and power have been acquired through devoted and concentrated effort, who are called upon for help.

The rNying-ma Sangha, with both married and celibate lamas, has successfully founded new centers in India, Nepal, Bhutan, and Sikkim, all maintaining the practice and tradition of the Ancient Ones. It is vitally important that the rNying-ma and all of the other traditions of Tibetan Buddhism in Tibet continue, so that the Dharma teachings as a whole may survive and prosper for the benefit of all beings.

The Marriage of Srong-btsan-sgam-po

Written by Srong-btsan-sgam-po himself and concealed for rediscovery at a later time, the Maṇi-bka'-'bum is part historical record and part Dharma teaching for the Tibetan people. It is one of the earliest surviving Tibetan works. These two selections, adapted from the Tibetan, relate to the marriage between Srong-btsan-sgam-po and Princess 'Un-shing Kong-jo of China, considered an emanation of Tārā.

Oṁ Maṇi Padme Hūṁ!

Having questioned King Srong-btsan-sgam-po about how to invite the Princess of China to Tibet, the minister mGar, guardian of the land, went to China with three hundred horsemen.

He already knew how to please the heart of the Chinese king: As the price for the Chinese princess, he brought a magic helmet made of precious beryl. Arriving at the emperor's court, he presented the helmet, saying:

"When engaged in battle, wear this helmet, and you will be victorious. When epidemics arise, circle the city wearing this helmet, and the sickness will be cut short. When there is fear of a bad harvest, circle the fields in it, and you will avert a poor crop. You will not find another helmet like this in the south. Offering this gift to the emperor, I beg your highness to give the princess in marriage to the King of Tibet." mGar also offered gifts of gold, casks, and money.

But the princess was not pleased, and the rest of the royal family plotted to prevent the marriage.

The emperor's son said, "All my older brothers have been killed by the Tibetans. My armies have been destroyed by the Tibetans. I have no enemy other than the Tibetans. I would rather give the princess to Gesar. Gesar is skilled and brave, and skill in military command is necessary in bad times." Speaking thus, he sent a message to Gesar.

The princess' mother said, "We are too wealthy for the Tibetans to compensate us for our daughter. Since a king without wealth is like a beggar, I will give the princess to the Persians instead, for they are very wealthy, and when bad times come, provisions are necessary." So she sent a messenger to the Persians.

The princess thought to herself. "Although it is necessary for me to go to a great man, the man himself is what is important. The king of Khrom is handsome, so I will go to the country of Khrom." And so she also sent a messenger.

The emperor said, "The Dharma has come from India. In recognition of this, I will give the princess to the king of India." And he sent a messenger. No one spoke in favor of the Tibetans.

By the next month, five hundred knights, the suitors of the princess, had gathered. The Tibetans said, "Since we have spoken for her first, we claim the princess."

But the men of Hor said to the emperor, "If you do not give the princess to us, Gesar will invade your country."

The Persians said, "If you do not give us the princess, we will burn your kingdom."

The king of Khrom had come himself, since he was so handsome. "If you do not give her to us," his men said, "we will overrun your kingdom."

Although no one favored the Tibetans, the law could not be swayed, so the emperor devised a series of tests and told the ministers that he would give the princess to the most ingenious minister among them.

The emperor had a very large turquoise with a small opening on its side and another opening underneath. The two were connected by a tiny, twisting tunnel. "To the one who can pass a piece of silk through the turquoise, I will give the princess."

The Tibetan minister mGar said, "You four ministers, the emperor thinks highly of you. See if your great powers can cause the silk to pass through the turquoise."

Having collected awls and pig bristles and all sorts of thread, each minister tried. The turquoise went from hand to hand, but no one could penetrate it. So the turquoise was given to mGar.

mGar had nurtured a Chinese ant. He attached to its waist a thread from a silk scarf; to this thread he attached a thicker strand, to the strand he attached a thick thread, and then the scarf itself. He put the ant into the lower hole and blew on it. Chased by the breath, the ant fled, arriving at the opening on the side. Gently pulling the different threads of silk, one by one, the minister made the scarf pass through. But in spite of this, the emperor did not want to give him the princess.

mGar then showed that he knew how to recognize and properly pair up one hundred mother birds and their one hundred chicks by sprinkling malt. But in spite of this, the emperor did not want to give him the princess.

mGar then showed that he knew how to recognize and properly pair up one hundred mares and their foals by giving them the appropriate thing. But in spite of this, the emperor still refused to give him the princess.

mGar then showed that he knew how to recognize the base and summit of a tree trunk by throwing it to the bottom of a lake. But the emperor still refused. And there were any number of contests: Who could eat a whole sheep? Who could drink the most beer? Who was the best with a cudgel? No one could beat the Tibetan. But even though he claimed the princess, she was still refused him.

Then, one night, a great gong was sounded. The governesses of the princess said, "Let the princess' suitors come to the palace." And the four other groups ran ahead. But the Tibetan ministers, having thought it over, decided that it was a trick. They marked the doors to their dwelling with vermilion letters, and put vajras on the lintels; counting the doorways, they made a mark on each one on their way to the palace.

When they arrived at the palace, the emperor told them, "Now, without making a mistake about the street, return to your dwellings. I will give my daughter to the one who recognizes his own house."

The other ministers became confused and could not find their way. But mGar, leading the Tibetan ministers and holding a lamp, followed the marks and led each Tibetan minister to his house. When the Chinese came to check on them, the other groups were lost, while the Tibetans had found their homes. And so they claimed the princess.

"Partiality would no longer be fitting," said the emperor. "Tomorrow, three hundred ladies will present themselves. To whoever recognizes the princess, she will be given."

mGar had won over a Chinese governess of the princess by gifts of food and clothing and by his attitude toward her. And he told her, "I will give you a measure of gold dust; for this, show me the princess. I will send her to Tibet and stay here myself to marry you."

But the governess objected. "The Chinese are skilled in divining such things," she said, "and they will cut off my head."

"I will prevent their divination," mGar said. He put a pan on a tripod, covered it with a net, and put it in a vase. He closed up the governess inside the vase. Passing a copper horn through the opening, he told the Chinese woman to speak through the horn.

"The princess will be dressed in seven-layered robes of rainbow colors. Each robe is shorter than the one just below it. Since she is so finely perfumed, a turquoise bee will be buzzing around her; between her eyebrows will be a red circle the size of a seed. Pass around her neck a silk scarf held by two vulture pinfeathers and lead her away."

The next day, the other four groups of ministers selected the best-dressed and prettiest ladies. But the Tibetans selected the princess, and using the feathers they led her away.

"Our wise sister and daughter is led away by the Tibetans!" said the Chinese, beating their breasts and wailing.

"There is nothing to be done," said the emperor. "Daughter, you must leave for Tibet."

"I won't find a single friend there," she complained. "There is neither Dharma nor wealth in Tibet. I won't go into that barbarous country."

Oṁ Maṇi Padme Hūṁ

When the princess asked her father for the Jo-bo-chen-po
to help her take the Dharma to Tibet, he replied:

"Out of love, my daughter,
I will give you the Jo-bo-chen-po,
the principal object of my adoration
and the very image of the Buddha,
said to resemble him in appearance.

"Whoever honors him,
and is full of love and compassion for all creatures,
and wishes that they all may attain liberation,
is promised supreme and rapid enlightenment.

"Whoever adores him,
weighed down with fear of endless rebirth,
wishing to be delivered this very moment,
will be saved and released from the fetters of existence.

"Whoever venerates him
in order to be saved from the tortures of hell
is promised the Blessed Paradise
after his suffering has been exhausted.

"Whoever desires the joys of this world,
if he prays to Jo-bo-chen-po
and brings offerings,
will see his desires realized.

"All those who bow to Jo-bo-chen-po with faith,
or with confidence make him a respectful offering,
or circumambulate him in contemplation
will quickly become Buddhas.

"Honor him with faith and respect!
It is this exceptional statue

that I give you out of love,
even though it seems to break my heart."

Her father also gave her treasures of jewels and ornaments, silks and furs, leaves from the Tree of Paradise, books on divination and magic, calendars, remedies, and dictionaries, as well as rules for governing monasteries and instructions and practices from Sūtras and Tantras.

All the preparations were finished for the departure of the Imperial Princess for Tibet, and the Jo-bo-chen-po was placed in the chariot. When the princess was ready to meet the Tibetan ministers, her father praised her to the assembled crowd:

"E Ma Ho!

"This virgin daughter named 'Un-shing
surpasses all the worldly arts by her perfection.
However many songs and dances there are in all
   the universe,
she knows them all without exception.
Whether you see her from the back or the front,
she is always beautiful.
Free from passions, anger, and frivolity,
she wishes to be of service to others,
and thus she is worthy of respect from all the universe.

"The Imperial Princess is a divine incarnation of Tārā;
having no equal in the world of men,
she is a fitting match for the Dharma king of Tibet,
who is an incarnation of Avalokiteśvara."

At the moment when the eastern stars reached the western sky, before the cry of the crow, the princess in her chariot, the Jo-bo-chen-po, and five hundred ministers on horseback departed for Tibet.

The princess reached Khams and stopped to wait for mGar to meet her, but he did not come. She went on to Zab-zing and lDan-ma, where she engraved the first volume of the Prajñāpāramitā into rock. Then she traveled to the forest of Sum-pa, in A-mdo province, where she was joined by mGar. He sent a courier ahead with this message:

"The princess and the divine Jo-bo-chen-po
are arriving in Central Tibet from the four directions.
May all Tibetans beat the drum
and fly the flags of celebration."

The Tibetan king had also sent forth a proclamation:

"Since the princess is a divine incarnation of Tārā, we do not know how she will arrive. Repair all the mountain roads and make ready for her approach."

Indeed, it seemed that she arrived in lHa-sa from all the four directions. Years later, the people of the east would talk about how she came through the grotto of Mal-dro. The proof was that they still call the ford in the river, The Passage of the Chinese Lady. The people of the south said that she came through Drib-phu, and that she called the glacier there The Conch, the name that remains to this day. The people of the west said she came through the lower valley of sTod-lung, and that it was she who fashioned the design of protection on the rocks where the deity lCam-srin resides. The northerners said that she came through the high pass of 'Phan-yul, and that forever after the town there has been called Bedecked with Flags, since her way had been paved that day with flying banners.

As the princess approached lHa-sa, she realized that the kingdom of Tibet was like a demon sleeping on its back and that the plain where lHa-sa had been built was in fact a palace of the nāga king. But she saw to the east a mountain like a bouquet of lotuses, to the south a mountain like a pile of jewels, to the west a mountain like a series of stūpas, and to the north a mountain like a shell on a tripod. She knew men of faith would come in great numbers from these places. If she built a sanctuary on the stūpa of 'Bum-thang,

NYINGMA INSTITUTE
1815 HIGHLAND PL.
BERKELEY, CA 94709
07/10/2018
14:34:08
DEBIT CARD
DEBIT SALE
Card #   XXXXXXXXXXXX3838
Network: VISA
Chip Card: US DEBIT
AID: A0000000980840
ATC: 0186
ARQC: DA55CFE5AFCE9832
SEQ #:
Batch #:   1
INVOICE   471
Approval Code: 1
Entry Method: 173945
Mode: Chip Read
Issuer - PIN Verified

SALE AMOUNT $22.94

CUSTOMER COPY

d virtue alone would fill all of Tibet.
e the crowd of faithful men would
esidence of the king would be con-
w where the many monks would con-
e would be built there. She saw where
would assemble and that a monastery
re. And there, in a happy place, would
ple.

e began to work on the place for the
pot, eight kinds of virtuous power are
ere are eight kinds of virtue, there will
of bad influences. The eight virtuous
unded on the eight petals of the terres-
eight spokes of the celestial wheel above.
iness would make four jewels in the four

new that in order to activate the power of
es, five of the eight opposing forces must
...st be destroyed. These five were the palace of the nāga king, the demon council, the resting place of the demon Ma-mo, the travel route of the evil spirits, and the hostile forces of the land. Setting out to destroy these forces one by one, she knew that she had to crush the nāga palace through the terrible power of the Jo-bo-chen-po. She placed the statue in the exact center of the kingdom, where it would press down upon the palace of the nāgas. Then she erected columns in each of the four directions around the Jo-bo-chen-po, wrapped a white silken cord around them, and hung a satin tent above the statue. At her bidding, two giants kept watch on the tent.

Thus 'Un-shing quickly began her work for the welfare of the Tibetan people. When she entered the gates of lHa-sa, the people danced with great joy, for the Jo-bo-chen-po had come to Tibet.

rNying-ma Lineage Holders

The rNying-ma lineage originates with the Ādibuddha Samantabhadra and enters human history through King Indrabhūti and dGa'-rab-rdo-rje, who transmitted the living traditions to their disciples. These teachings passed down through great enlightened masters including Guru Padma-sambhava, Vimalamitra, and Buddhaguhya, who brought them to Tibet.

The lineage includes Mantrayāna teachings which are preserved only in the rNying-ma school. These are the three Inner Tantras: the Mahā, the Anu, and the Atiyoga, or rDzogs-chen. If these lineages were to disappear, a unique source of enlightened knowledge would vanish from the face of the earth.

Each Inner Tantra has its own lineage holders, and the list given here is by no means complete. However, anyone seriously interested in the rNying-ma teachings will wish to learn more about the great masters portrayed here, whose teachings hold open the door to enlightenment now and for generations to come.

Kun-tu-bzang-po The personification of the unmanifest Dharmakāya.

rDo-rje-sems-dpa' *The personification of Sambhogakāya, the symbol of purity and bliss.*

dGa'-rab-rdo-rje   The Nirmāṇakāya manifestation of rDo-rje-sems-dpa', first of the Atiyoga (rDzogs-chen) lineage in human form.

'Jam-dpal-bshes-gnyen A master of all nine yānas; the direct successor of dGa'-rab-rdo-rje.

Śrī Siṁha   Third holder of the Atiyoga or rDzogs-chen lineage and the teacher of Padmasambhava.

Ye-shes-mdo   In the direct lineage of Śrī Siṁha; holder of most of the esoteric doctrines of the Atiyoga.

Padmasambhava   The lotus-born Oḍḍiyāna guru, founder of Tibetan Buddhism. Born four or twelve years after the Parinirvāṇa of the Buddha.

Vimalamitra   An outstanding Indian mahāpaṇḍita from Oḍḍiyāna who mastered the Tripiṭaka and studied with Śrī Siṁha in China before transmitting the Atiyoga teachings to Tibet.

Śāntarakṣita Invited to Tibet, this great paṇḍita founded bSam-yas together with King Khri-srong-lde-btsan and Padmasambhava and ordained the first Tibetan monks.

Khri-srong-lde-btsan The eighth-century Tibetan king and patron of Buddhism who invited Padmasambhava to Tibet. One of Padmasambhava's twenty-five principal disciples.

Ye-shes-mtsho-rgyal Tibet's foremost female teacher and one of Padma-sambhava's closest disciples, who mastered his complete teachings and preserved them for future generations.

Vairotsana Prominent eighth-century Tibetan vidyādhara and translator, one of Padmasambhava's most accomplished disciples.

gNubs-chen Sangs-rgyas-ye-shes   One of the earliest rNying-ma bKa'-ma masters, a vital link in the lineage of the Lotus-Born Guru.

Zur-po-che An accomplished siddha and vidyādhara, bearer of many Mantrayāna lineages.

Rong-zom Chos-kyi-bzang-po A *highly accomplished eleventh-century rNying-ma scholar.*

Klong-chen-rab-'byams-pa The fourteenth-century master accorded the title All-Knowing, the supreme lama of the rNying-ma tradition.

*O-rgyan gTer-bdag-gling-pa   Great gTer-ma master of the seventeenth century;
student and teacher of the Fifth Dalai Lama.*

Lo-chen Dharmaśrī The brother of gTer-bdag-gling-pa, learned and versed in all branches of knowledge. He systematized the practices of the three yānas.

'Jigs-med-gling-pa Eighteenth-century rDzogs-chen master and a manifestation of Klong-chen-pa; founder of the Klong-chen-snying-thig tradition in its systematic form. On passing away, he had three reincarnations.

'Jigs-med-rgyal-ba'i-myu-gu   Direct disciple of 'Jigs-med-gling-pa and guru of
dPal-sprul Rinpoche; one of the 'Four 'Jigs-med' who continued the lineage of
their master.

rGyal-sras gZhan-phan-mtha'-yas   The foremost scholar of his time. Abbot of rDzogs-chen monastery, he gave new life to the study of Buddhist philosophy in the province of Khams, in eastern Tibet.

mDo-mkhyen-brtse Ye-shes-rdo-rje The heart incarnation of 'Jigs-med-gling-pa and a great siddha.

dPal-sprul Rinpoche (b. 1808) The speech incarnation of 'Jigs-med-gling-pa.
A leader in the nineteenth-century ris-med movement.

'Jam-dbyangs-mkhyen-brtse'i-dbang-po (b. 1820) The body incarnation of 'Jigs-med-gling-pa, he was one of the founders of the non-sectarian ris-med movement, holding the lineages of all major schools. He authored fifteen volumes of Sūtra and Tantra commentary.

'Jam-mgon Blo-gros-mtha'-yas (dKong-sprul) (b. 1813) The most accomplished of 'Jam-dbyangs-mkhyen-brtse's disciples. He compiled Five Treasures, one of which is the Rin-chen-gter-mdzod, a compilation of gTer-ma teachings in 63 volumes.

Lama Mi-pham (b. 1846) An unexcelled rNying-ma scholar, an incarnation of Mañjuśrī and an authority in all fields of knowledge, known also for his spiritual achievements.

A-'dzom 'brug-pa A disciple of 'Jams-dbyangs-mkhyen-brtse, dPal-sprul Rinpoche, and Lama Mi-pham. He completely mastered the sNying-thig lineage teachings and passed on his realization to many disciples.

The Seven Gurus
of Tarthang Tulku

With the encouragement of his first teachers, Tarthang Tulku traveled widely in Tibet, seeking out the great masters of the day. Journeying from monastery to monastery to study with great lineage holders who manifested the awakened realization of higher consciousness, he received an unusually broad and deep education in the major lineages of the Tibetan Buddhist tradition. Often he was the youngest among those receiving teachings. Today, as the lamas able to transmit these lineages grow old and pass away, he is almost unique in being able to transmit a wide spectrum of powerful teachings.

Although Tarthang Tulku had twenty-five major teachers in all, he considers the seven masters portrayed here the gurus who communicated to him the heart of the rNying-ma teachings. Their blessings have sustained him in all of the work he has undertaken in the West.

'Jam-dbyangs-mkhyen-brtse Chos-kyi-blo-gros (b. 1893)   The reincarnation of 'Jam-dbyangs-mkhyen-brtse'i-dbang-po and incarnation of Padmasambhava; the most excellent teacher during the first half of this century. In the ris-med tradition, his teachings to Tarthang Tulku include the Sūtras, higher philosophy, Vajrayāna meditation, and extensive initiations and instructions in the higher Tantras.

His Holiness Dar-thang mChog-sprul Chos-kyi-zla-ba (b. 1893) An incarnation of Mañjuśrī and the supreme abbot of Dar-thang Monastery in 'Gu-log. The most excellent example of a Buddhist master, he was the founder of many monasteries. His teachings to Tarthang Tulku include personal meditation instruction and many sNying-thig initiations.

Venerable Zhe-chen dKong-sprul (b. 1901) The second 'Jam-mgon Blo-gros-mtha'-yas. His teachings to Tarthang Tulku consist of the Sūtras and secret esoteric Tantras, the thirteen volumes of Zhe-chen rGyal-tshab, the thirty-two volumes of the collected works of Lama Mi-pham, the rgyud-long-ma-sngags, and meditation instruction.

Padma Siddhi (b. 1888) An incarnation of Avalokiteśvara and Srong-btsan-sgam-po, who emphasized practice of the six-syllable mantra. His teachings to Tarthang Tulku included great perfection meditation, initiation, and Bodhisattva ordination.

rGyal-sras 'Gyur-med-rdo-rje (b. 1895) The son of A-'dzom-'brug-pa and an incarnation of O-rgyan gTer-bdag-gling-pa. His teachings include dGongs-pa-zang-thal, sNying-thig practices and studies, many Tantra commentaries, and Mahāsaṁdhi Yoga.

sNang-mdzad-grub-pa'i-rdo-rje A Vajrapāṇi incarnation and abbot of Zhe-chen Monastery, also known as the Sixth Zhe-chen Rab-'byams. His teachings to Tarthang Tulku include the sixty-three volume Rin-chen-gter-mdzod initiation and teachings, thousands of initiations and practices, and rDzogs-chen meditation.

mDo-sngags-bstan-pa'i-nyi-ma (b. 1907) Foremost successor in the line of Lama Mi-pham, teacher at Kaḥ-thog Monastery, and renowned author. He studied thirty-seven years under Kun-bzang-dpal-ldan. His teachings to Tarthang Tulku include Sūtras and śāstras, commentaries on the sGyu-'phrul-gsang-ba'i-snying-po, and rDzogs-chen meditation.

Part Two

Teachings from
the Tradition

Orienting the Mind to the Dharma

Klong-chen-pa

The appearance of this life is like a waking dream.

Introduction

Until the fourteenth century, writings about the sacred, secret teachings in Tibet remained obscure and difficult of access. At this time, however, one of the most renowned and learned masters of the rNying-ma lineage, Kun-mkhyen Klong-chen-rab-'byams-pa (1308–1364) wrote a number of concise and lucid texts on Mahāyoga, Anuyoga, and Atiyoga. Despite the depth and complexity of these subjects, Klong-chen-pa's presentation was exceptionally clear and understandable. His work helped to define many of the essential doctrines and practices of the rNying-ma school.

Although he was the abbot of bSam-yas monastery early in his life, Klong-chen-pa retired from monastic life to live simply in the mountains of Tibet. There he prepared his most profound works, among the most perfect renderings of philosophical and psychological truths ever collected. These are referred to as the sNying-thig, works that systematically explain the teachings of rDzogs-chen, Path of Absolute Perfection. The mDzod-bdun, or Seven Treasures, as well as many other of his writings, subdivide the rDzogs-chen (Atiyoga) system, discussing and explaining the inner, outer, and secret meanings of sādhana practices, oral teachings, and initiation.

Klong-chen-pa's knowledge was so vast as to be incomprehensible to the ordinary mind. The title Kun-mkhyen means all-knowing and indicates the extent of Klong-chen-pa's achievement. Through his instruction, many of his disciples attained enlightenment.

In his Jeweled Garland of Four Topics, Klong-chen-pa describes how one can "enter the refreshing shade of the Conqueror's teachings, a wish-fulfilling tree." He describes this process of release from suffering in four chapters: Orienting the Mind to the Dharma, Traversing the Dharma Path, Removing Error on the Path, and Purifying Error into Wisdom. The first chapter is presented here.

Homage to all Buddhas and Bodhisattvas!
With vast faith I bow to the sun-like Sugata,
who in the vast expanse of space,
Dharmakāya,
opens the mandala of Nirmāṇakāya,
endowed with the five certainties:
the smiling lotus of those to be trained
with the light-rays of his action.

Pray listen as I explain the four kinds of sublime qualities: the way those who have faith gradually enter the cooling shade of the wish-fulfilling tree of the Conqueror's teachings, which offers refuge from suffering and relief from worldly existence.

Those who wish to cross the ocean of boundless existence must first consider: "If I am to achieve true happiness, the peace of the teaching of liberation, I must begin to strive in this very lifetime. I must start today.

"If I do not make an effort while I have the leisure and opportunity and this human body, a vessel so hard to gain and easy to lose, I will never be freed from the ocean of existence or be able to cut off the stream of its endless, diverse forms of suffering."

The other shore of the river of birth and death is not visible. Yet you frolic in this fearful, unbearable lake, everywhere disturbed by the froth of sickness and old age, its troubled waves of emotionality washing over the very peaks of existence.

Having heard these words, cut the stream of birth and old age, and you will never be separated from great bliss. With the precious boat of the Supreme Dharma, strive to cross over the troubled ocean of the three worlds.

If you do not establish the enlightened path of liberation today, later you will not even hear the words 'happy existence'. As you endlessly move from one bad existence to the next, what chance will arise to be freed from samsara?

Therefore, while you are fortunate enough to have human existence, if you have sense, you will strive from the heart! Achieving happiness and benefit, you will realize the true value of your own being and that of others.

If you have this opportune occasion, but lack a steadfast mind, earnestly reflect, "All things are unstable, without essence, momentary, impermanent, and subject to decay: I too will soon die."

When the world, this vessel of life, is consumed seven times by fire, one time by water, and then scattered to the wind, not even the tip of a hair will remain. All will be empty, one with the sky.

The essence of life is impermanent, moving and changing. All sentient beings, be they gods, asuras, men, animals, hungry ghosts, or hell beings, are sunk in the river of birth and death until the end of time.

Years, months, and seasons, days and moments perish and move on. The changing seasons bring grief. Always there is some loss. Think how fleeting is your own life.

The mind is not stable! Life is easily parted from the body. It is uncertain which will come first, tomorrow or the end of your life. From this day forward, keep this in mind.

But fear the suffering of birth even more than death. Wherever you are born, you will have no true joy. The nature of samsara is like a fiery pit. We must seek the means to free ourselves today!

Hell beings suffer from heat and cold; hungry ghosts from hunger and thirst; animals from being eaten by one another. Human beings are plagued by many difficulties. The asuras fight and the gods plunge into death.

When joy turns into pain, there is great suffering. Consider falling from the blissful delights of heaven into the fires of hell; then strive to cross beyond existence!

The appearance of this life is like a waking dream. Leaving behind what is changing and impermanent, you must move on. What good is samsara with its pleasures? Right now, you must strive for the Dharma!

Desire is like poison, a sword, or fire. When engrossed in desire, there is no place for joy. Made miserable by accumulating, hoarding, and guarding, you are forever shackled by pride, avarice, and greed.

When you contend with everyone, the defiling emotions increase. Agitated by entertainments, body and life force grow restless. The Exalted Ones scorn this striving to do and to be.

With few desires, virtues naturally increase. Those who enter the liberating path of peace reduce desire and are content. The one who has exhausted desire is said to be truly exalted, while the one with few desires belongs to the family of the Exalted Ones.

In the same way that desires increase emotional turbulence and suffering, diminishing desires increases happiness. Those who follow the sublime beings of the past should always be satisfied with just enough.

Immeasurable are the difficulties arising from associating with others! Great are the obligations and agitations of meaningless activities. Anger and aggression increase, leading to obsessive hatred.

Caught in meaningless involvements, you are always tainted with suffering. Whatever is done is joyless. Even if you have been taught, benefit is rare. Even if you have listened, you still lack the Dharma.

In the end, the dearest friends are parted. Leave your loving friends, relatives, and associates behind! Proceed alone to achieve the sacred Dharma.

From this day forward, commit yourself! The excellent, holy ones of the past are said to have found the nectar of the Dharma while alone. To establish inner peace, go also in solitude to the forest.

The Conquerors have praised solitude, for in the unpeopled wilderness meditation deepens, and as disgust for what is impermanent grows, the Dharma is naturally realized.

Undistracted by entertainments or the care of possessions, you will find faith and grow weary with the world; many good qualities will arise. Without entanglements, you have little to do. Unconcerned about the opinions of others, you are protected from praise and blame, pleasure and pain, elation and depression, loss and gain.

In dense forests, completely alone, you will achieve profound meditation. Day and night will be spent with the Dharma in happiness and freedom. As the meaningful opportunity that life presents is put to use for the sake of realization, qualities of inexpressible excellence come into being.

May the refreshing rain
of well-expressed Dharma
thus relieve the torment of troubling emotions,
completely filling the lotus lake
of virtue and meditation;
increasing inner wealth in the land of peace.

A complete translation of this work has appeared as *The Four-Themed Precious Garland* (Dharamsala: Library of Tibetan Works and Archives, 1979); reprinted in S. Batchelor, *The Jewel in the Lotus* (London: Wisdom Publications, 1987).

How to Hear the Teachings

dPal-sprul Rinpoche

*Without overly tightening the mind and withdrawing
it inward, moderate tightness and looseness.*

Introduction

dPal-sprul Rinpoche (1808–1887), whose full name was 'Jigs-med-chos-kyi-dbang-phyug, was born into a nomadic family in Dza-chu-kha, in 'Gu-log in eastern Tibet. He studied with great masters of all the schools, including the fourth rDzogs-chen Rinpoche, 'Jigs-med-rgyal-ba'i-myu-gu and mDo-Khyen-brtse Ye-shes-rdo-rje, one of the three incarnations of 'Jigs-med-gling-pa. Considered an emanation of Śāntideva, the renowned seventh-century siddha and author of the Bodhi-caryāvatāra, he placed great emphasis on direct, practical advice that could be applied by people at all levels of attainment. He emphasized study of the Bodhicaryāvatāra and chanting of the sacred mantra of Avalokiteśvara.

Trained originally as a monk, dPal-sprul Rinpoche left the monastery to take up the life of a hermit and spent many years wandering throughout 'Gu-log, giving teachings to those he met on his travels. Later he returned to rDzogs-chen monastery to teach, but he spent the last part of his life in the Dza-chu-kha valley. There he constructed a great Maṇi Wall extending for more than a mile and said to contain 100,000 stones, on each of which was inscribed the mantra Oṁ Maṇi Padme Hūṁ.

This selection was adapted from the first chapter of dPal-sprul Rinpoche's Kun-bzang-bla-ma'i-zhal-lung, a summary of the rDzogs-chen-snying-thig teachings and an introduction to the practice of Vajrayāna. For over a century, this work has been beloved throughout Tibet for its many stories and its simple statement of profound teachings.

Whenever you hear or explain the teachings, or meditate and accomplish the teachings, give up these three: remembering the past, passionate interest in the future, and losing yourself in present objects of thought.

Take to heart these words of rGyal-sras Rinpoche:

Vanished!
That which is past history
(the pleasure, the pain),
like images composed on water
vanishes at the end point.
Once it is gone,
do not thereafter reflect on it.

Memories
(when they do follow):

Use them to consider
how good and bad times gather together
only to be swept away.

What hope but Dharma, Mantra-Reciter?

Plotting the future
is fishing in a parched ravine.
Hold fast from abstract speculations,
from wishing and craving.

Reflect
(should such thoughts persist)
that death arrives unheralded.

What time will you allot the world,
Mantra-Reciter?

Present upkeep is like
doing housekeeping in a dream.
Useless! Stop!
The sustenance required for practice
comes wrapped in non-attachment.

The local bustle is hollow, Mantra-Reciter.

When not meditating,
trim your thoughts,
lance the three poisons,
till all appearance
is regarded as Dharmakāya.
This is the method:
Bear it in mind when apt.

Why cling to errant thoughts, Mantra-Reciter?

As the adage has it:
'Be unconcerned with concerns that are not yet'.
Too hasty a reach for the future guarantees
that the fate of Moon Fame's father shall be ours.

In the past a poor man found a large quantity of barley in a deserted shed. Pouring it into a bag, he hung it from the ceiling. Then he lay down under the bag and began to think: "Based on this barley, great fortune will come to me! I will take a wife, and surely a son will be born." As he began to wonder what to name the child, the moon rose. "I will call him Moon Fame," he exclaimed.

While he was daydreaming in this way, a mouse was eating through the rope that held the bag of barley. The rope gave way, the bag fell on top of him, and he was killed.

There is no time to rely on the many strings of thoughts about the future or the past. Since they only disturb your stream of consciousness, you should give them up and listen to the teachings attentively and carefully.

Another problem comes if you remember and raise excessive points from each and every word and meaning of the teaching. Then you will be like a bear catching mice: When you grasp one, the others will be forgotten. You will never understand much this way. Yet if you are too withdrawn, there is the problem of falling into sleep and dullness. So tightness and looseness should be moderated.

In the past Ānanda was teaching meditation to Śroṇakoṭi. Yet Śroṇakoṭi could not generate proper meditation because he was sometimes too tight and sometimes too loose. So he questioned the Buddha, who replied, "Were you skilled at playing the violin when you were a householder?"

"Very skilled," Śroṇakoṭi replied.

"Did the sound of your violin come from very loose strings or from very tight strings?"

"Indeed, neither of these were appropriate. The sound came from a moderation of tightness and looseness."

"Your mind should also be like that."

From these words Śroṇakoṭi attained the fruit of the path.

Ma-gcig Lab-sgron-ma has said:

Hold fast with alertness
and relax with looseness.
This is the core of the view.

Without overly tightening the mind and withdrawing it inward, moderate tightness and looseness.

[Also,] do not be discouraged during long periods of hearing the teaching due to hunger, thirst, or other minor discomforts caused by the wind, sun, rain, and so on. Listen joyfully and with delight, thinking:

"Now I have attained a precious human body. I have met a qualified teacher. What joy to hear his profound instructions! I can hear the teaching now only because I collected merit for countless aeons. This occasion is like being able to eat the food of an entire lifetime at one time. Thus, for the sake of the teachings I will endure whatever discomforts of heat and cold might arise."

The Teaching of the Essential Point in Three Words

Lama Mi-pham

By experiencing within, one understands.

Introduction

Lama Mi-pham (Mi-pham 'Jam-dbyangs rnam-rgyal rgya-mtsho, The Completely Victorious Ocean of Gentle Voice, 1846–1912) was the most renowned scholar in Tibet during the nineteenth century. Born near the Khams border in 'Gu-log, in eastern Tibet, he was educated amidst the spiritual ferment and regeneration of the nineteenth century ris-med movement, which collected theories and techniques from many lineages. These were arranged and taught as different and/or alternate stages in the process of development.

Extremely catholic in his interests, Lama Mi-pham made significant contributions to medicine, music, sculpture, engineering, mathematics, and astrology. He was also an accomplished yogi, deeply involved with experiments in telepathy, the effect of mantras, the control of inanimate matter, and the prediction of future lives. Nowadays, however, his fame rests chiefiy on his contribution to Dharma studies. He systematized the Sūtras and Tantras; he linked the various theories made available through the ris-med movement with those of Klong-chen-pa, reweaving the whole structure into a coherent and unified path. He compiled and practiced over two hundred sādhanas and at one time spent seven years in retreat.

Homage to Mañjuśrī

The understanding of ordinary people is defective.
Recognition itself is not disclosed by words.

Turning from what draws you in, grasp the refinement
   of what is to be done;
Doing thus, the facticity of mind is recognized.

Thought formation is not bound by tenseness;
likewise the fundamental continuity is self-contained,
since action, exertion, and the matrix of purposeful grasping
   do not exist.
Doing thus is the ongoing meditation.

Because the realm of voidness is like the clouds,
All the various thought formations are like their ebb
   and flow,
When pacified through lack of benefit or injury.
Doing thus is self-liberation.

This is the teaching of the essential point in three words. By experiencing within, one understands.

Set down by Mi-pham-rnam-par-rgyal-ba
on the third day of the month in the Fire-Monkey year.

Discussion

"The Teaching of the Essential Point in Three Words" sets down in very concise form the means by which self-liberation is attained. This is explained in three parts: the ground, the path, and the fruit.

The ground is threefold. One must realize that the understanding, knowledge, and teachings of ordinary, worldly people do not indicate truth. They are a deviation from truth. One must realize that awareness cannot be revealed or recognized through language—that recognition of reality is through experience. One must realize that in order to gain experience, attraction toward worldly pleasures and concerns must be abandoned, and one must perfect the work of gaining liberation. Upon accomplishing these, one gains insight into the fact of mind recognition. The essence of the ground is the facticity of mind.

The path is threefold. One must not become tense, tight, or bound but remain loose, calm, and free when thoughts appear, when disturbances arise, when discursive thought occurs. One must continue unwaveringly, because the fundamental continuity cannot be disturbed, cannot be affected by thought-formation; like an island, it is self-contained, and is timeless. One must realize the non-existence of deeds, of effortful striving, and of the source from which come all determined attempts to seize upon and hold any thoughts. Upon doing so, one learns the method of prolonged meditation. The essence of the path is the absence of the matrix of purposeful grasping.

The fruit is threefold. One recognizes that the emptiness of reality is not really different from the cloudedness of thought formations. One recognizes that the process of thought formation is like waves in the ocean. One recognizes indifference to these waves, knowing the mind to be empty of real entities. Thus the robber-like thoughts find nothing to steal and the helpful thoughts find no one to assist. Thereupon is found release from the cause of samsara; thereupon is attained the great self-liberation. The essence of the fruit is self-liberation.

Such is the teaching of the crucial point in three words. Those alone who gain recognition through experience can truly understand the great mystery.

The Mark
of the Mahāyāna

Śāntideva

*Come now, I invite you to Buddha nature, and, by
the way, to happiness.* —*Bodhicaryāvatāra*

Introduction

The mark of the Mahāyāna is a boundless love for all beings,
an intention to end all suffering and bring all beings to the
supreme joy of enlightenment, while also offering them happiness along the way. This is bodhicitta, the mind and heart
bent on complete illumination for every living creature.
Sometimes called the thought of enlightenment, bodhicitta
is far more than any ordinary thought. It is the mind transformed by intention into a vehicle of realization.

   The eighth-century master Śāntideva explored the nature
and practice of bodhicitta in the Bodhicaryāvatāra, one of

the most renowned works of the Mahāyāna tradition. These excerpts, adapted from the third and the tenth chapters of that work, praise bodhicitta and express its inner essence as it applies to the conventional world—the heartfelt wish that the merit and benefit of practice contribute to the welfare of all beings.

Buddhas of the past
generated the thought of enlightenment
and trained in the Bodhisattva path.

Like them I will manifest
the thought of enlightenment
for the benefit of all beings,
and will properly practice
the stages of the path.

Having considered and comprehended
the thought of enlightenment,
for growth and well-being
the wise should praise it like this:

Today my birth is complete;
the fruit of life has ripened—
I am a Buddha-son.
My action shall be in harmony
with this faultless family.

A jewel in a dust heap,
found by a blind man—
this thought of enlightenment
has arisen in me.

It is
the alchemy that transforms death,
the treasure that transmutes poverty,
the cure that stops the world's disease.

Deeply rooted,
it is a sheltering tree,
offering refuge from endless roaming about
in being.

When a chasm opens
on a difficult path
it is the bridge
that carries you across.

It is the full moon of mind
cooling the river of passion,
a great sun pushing away the darkness
of obscuring ignorance.

It is sweet butter
churning up
from the milk of Dharma.

Humanity, hungering for happiness
gone astray on the road of being:
This great feast is for you.
It will nurture all who partake.

Come now,
I invite you to Buddha nature,
and, by the way, to happiness.

In the presence of all the Protectors,
may the gods, the antigods,
and all others
rejoice.

Whatever merit is mine
I give it away to all beings.
May they be happy;
may they engage in the Bodhisattva practice.
I wish for all an ocean of delight.

May the joy of the Bodhisattva
stream forth without a break,
in all directions,
into all realms,
to as many beings as there are.

To as many hell-beings as there are:
Those suffering from cold—may they be warmed.
Those suffering from heat—may they be refreshed.
Sword-leaf trees: Turn into sandalwood forests!
Hail of embers: Turn into rain of flowers!
River of fire: Turn into the Holy Ganges!

O friends, come quickly!
Banish fear—awake!
The power of joy, freedom from all suffering,
complete protection—love and bodhicitta—
shall be generated in all beings.

To as many animals as there are:
May they be free from the fear
of being eaten by one another.

To as many hungry ghosts as there are:
May they be made content
by the stream of milk flowing forth
from noble Avalokiteśvara's hand.

To as many human beings as there are:
May the blind see and the deaf hear;
may the hungry be fed and the poor obtain wealth.
May the tormented find ease and the sick be cured;
may the frightened be unafraid
and the imprisoned be freed.

May the powerless gain power
and the wisdom to use it well.
And the demented, the drunk, the irrational,
and those in despair,

wandering in a pathless wilderness—
may they be watched over.

May kings govern according to the Dharma.
May good places of learning flourish.
May harvests be bounteous.
May all beings obtain the leisure,
wealth, and freedom required to practice.
May all beings abandon evil
and never be separated
from the thought of enlightenment.

May those who have gained bliss
not be content with less than complete enlightenment;
may those who have made mistakes
and lost confidence not despair—
may their confusion clear up.

May all beings live long lives.
May even the sound of the word 'death' perish.

May all the Buddhas be worshipped;
may all the Bodhisattvas accomplish their intentions.
Whatever they wish for the benefit of beings,
may beings have even that.

Mañjuśrī acts to bring forth the value
of all beings,
whose numbers extend to the end of the sky.
May my activity be like his.

As long as space exists,
as long as beings exist,
for that long,
may I remove the suffering of beings.

A Ladder to Liberation

dPal-sprul Rinpoche

The following selection was adapted from the Chos-dang-'jigs-rten shes-pa'i bstan-bcos gdol-ba'i-drang-srong-gi-gtam thar-pa'i-them-skas ("A Ladder to Liberation").

That which is called a continuous self
cannot be found
outside of thought.
We are bound to the appearance of samsara
simply by thought;
we are bound to its transcendence
simply by thought.

Virtue and sin are only thoughts;
path and error are thoughts;
self and selflessness: thoughts.

Systems and schools, all are thoughts.
Taming thought is the essence,
expressing the supreme significance of all teachings,
past and present.

If you ask how thoughts are tamed:
First classify, second examine, third put to rest.

Thoughts are classified white or black.
Confidence, the mind set on enlightenment,
and penetrating awareness are white.
Desire, hatred, and ignorance are black.
Expand the white!
Clear up the black!

White points toward perfection:
complete virtue, present and future.
Black points toward sin: complete evil,
present and future.

Confidence unites your wholesome intentions;
mind set on enlightenment is the ground
of the Bodhisattva's path.
Penetrating awareness is the root
of every path to freedom.
Produce these three!

Desire grasps at worldly existence;
hatred produces misery;
ignorance is the soil
that bears the fruit of desire and hatred.
Abandon these three!

Confidence in the sublime Dharma,
a mind set on enlightenment that desires
Buddhahood for the benefit of others,
penetrating awareness that realizes
the illusory character of all things—

these three purify what poisons
our being and obscures the light.

Now, to examine thoughts:
Ever mindful of what is important,
guarding the blazing fire of awareness,
whenever you are selfishly involved,
look at your own face!
Merely seeing, there is openness:
No need for further analysis.

Insubstantial, fleeting, unsettled—
thoughts are naturally open,
and the nature of openness
is self-knowing radiance.
Knowing the openness of mind in this way,
you know the openness of all things.
No need to examine everything.
If you sever the root of a tree,
the branches soon dry out.

Mind is the root of all things,
and so the openness of mind makes all things open.
This direct seeing of self-openness
does not give rise to further analysis.
At last one meets one's mind face to face:
Beyond expression, beyond thought;
nothing stored up, nothing tied down.
We say, "radiant light!"

Now to put to rest:
Realizing meaning devoid of specifics,
experiencing states not tied to anything,
who will know realization or non-realization?
Where will one look for the one who realizes,
or for that which is realized?

No need now to abandon thoughts,
to purify, to practice,

to travel the path and become free.
Settled in freshness, free in its own state:
at the time of appearance, openness;
at the time of openness, appearance.

Appearance and openness—no divisions—
radiant light, unhindered luminous compassion.
Subject and object—self-liberating—
radiance of mind and primordial wisdom.
Subject-object not two:
mind set on enlightenment and the ultimately real
arise as a pair.
Seeing this truth:
Great Bliss.

One Flavor

dPal-sprul Rinpoche

In the unified matrix
of pure awareness,
birth and death
have one flavor.

We live delighting in obsession,
deceived by illusion,
running after phantoms.
People and things appear in the mind
as the moon appears in water.
Seeing this, what is myriad
has one flavor.

Knowing the cold flesh of old age,
we long for the fresh fires of youth.
Releasing our attitudes about the body
into the limitless realm,

old age and youth
have one flavor.

The tighter we hold
the objects of obsession,
the greater the suffering of death.
In the unified matrix of pure awareness,
birth and death
have one flavor.

Unfulfilled longing
for the affection that joined us with another
compels further action.
Breaking this pattern
that just spins around,
meetings and partings
have one flavor.

We desire birth as a god;
fear we will fall into hell.
Divinity is embedded in existence!
Seeing this,
gods and demons
have one flavor.

Driven to extremes in pursuit of realization,
one task done, a hundred more arise.
Once we know non-divisive mind,
it is sufficient to relax
in the flavor of effortlessness.

Following everyone's instructions,
your activities will be endless.
Cut your own cord!
That will bind all trivial inclinations.

Although others see great good,
if you know your own fault,
it's meaningless to pretend you're good.

The flavor of the fault
will conceal the value.

Attending to what is meaningful,
a fox can become king.
If it spends its time in trivialities,
it will just rake the mud in its den.

If you act only on beautiful words,
you won't see the rough places to come.
Know your own limitations,
how far you can go!
Then beautiful words and difficult times
are like food and clothing:
Both essential
for crossing the mountain pass.

Ha Ha
That's all I'm going to say!

He He
Whatever arises that's meaningless:
Cut it short!

Ho Ho
This is by dPal-sprul.

The Four Demons

Ma-gcig Lab-sgron-ma

One of many exceptional women who have attained liberation by following the path of the Mantrayāna, Ma-gcig Lab-sgron-ma was a twelfth-century follower of the gCod lineage brought to Tibet by her master, the great Pha-dam-pa-sangs-rgyas. In this selection from her works she gives instructions to her student Gan-pa-mug-sang.

Listen my son, and I will teach you the nature of demons. What we call a demon is very, very huge and colored all black. Whoever sees one is truly terrified and trembles from head to foot. But demons don't really exist!

The truth of the matter is this: Anything whatsoever that obstructs the attainment of liberation is a demon. Even loving and affectionate relatives can become demons if they hinder your practice. But the greatest demon of them all is the belief in a self as a lasting and independent principle. If you don't destroy this clinging to a self, the demons will just keep lifting you up and dropping you down. So you must practice wisely and diligently—destroy this demon 'Belief in a Self'!

Now there are three other kinds of demons that rise up associated with this ego-clinging, so in all there are four kinds of demons that must be destroyed. We can call them the tangible demons, the intangible demons, the demons of hedonistic delights, and the demons of subjectivity. But all of them are connected to belief in the self.

First let us consider the so-called tangible demons. The eye sees color and form. Color-forms that are judged to be pleasant create attraction, and color-forms judged to be ugly produce repulsion. The same thing happens when the ear hears, the nose smells, the tongue tastes, and the body experiences tactile sensations. Pleasant sense objects attract and unpleasant ones repel. But whether you are caught by desire or aversion, I tell you: They are demons!

This loving and hating objects as though they were real, this whole obsessive attitude toward sense perceptions—these are the very conditions that cause such suffering and misery to sentient beings. They bind all beings to the frustrating flow of constant becoming. For that reason they are called demons. And since these demons consist in believing that the pleasant or unpleasant sense objects are concrete and real, they are called tangible. My son, since all such attachments and obsessions with either good or bad are demons, destroy such attachments and obsessions!

Further, my child, consider this: Although the colors and forms we see are there as a presence, that very presence is itself nothing real. Although present, this structure has no abiding essence. You must understand: There can be no real acceptance or rejection of any kind of form in itself! True, you cannot stop the appearance of form, but you need not hang on to what is only appearance. By removing your in-

Ma-gcig Lab-sgron-ma, the great twelfth-century Tibetan yoginī.

fatuation with mere appearances, you are freed from the obstacles that come from color-form. And the same applies to sounds, smells, tastes, and bodily sensations.

I do hope that now you understand exactly how tangible things can be demons and how you can free yourself from them. As you are the child of this lineage, listen well, for now I will describe the intangible demons and how they operate. Pay attention, and keep this firmly in your mind!

We call them intangible demons because they don't appear concretely as objects of the senses. Rather, they are the manifold pleasant or unpleasant experiences that arise within the mind itself. Experiences that frighten or upset us we call devils, while pure experiences of gaiety and ebullience we call gods. If you embroil your mind in either of these, it is bound to become emotionally unstable. Although the emotions do not exist tangibly and do not manifest any substance as real, concrete objects, they still have a definite ability to harm you as you run here and there trying to adjust to them.

So again, they are called demons. And insofar as they have no abiding nature and are not present as tangible things, they are called intangible demons.

Now in fact, from the very beginning neither the good that we call gods nor the evil that we call devils, nor even the very mind that becomes so obsessed with beneficial or vicious qualities has ever really existed—not even so much as the tip of a hair! They are mere nothingness, free from any foundation.

Yet you must not repress these emotional obsessions, such as sentimentality and the like. Whatever experiences arise, whether good or bad, do not try to force them from your consciousness. Nor should you get involved in making up ideas about them and then getting stuck in your own concepts. Whatever thoughts or memories arise in your mind, just let them be.

All mental activities are simply the shining lucency of the great expanse of mind. This mind is like a great ocean: The ocean itself never goes anywhere, yet waves ripple across its surface. So whatever pleasant or unpleasant things arise, do not further stir them up by ruminating on them. If you just leave them alone, the intangible demons will disappear by themselves.

Now, my son, let us examine the behavior of the demons of hedonistic delights. Certain mental states have a rich and infatuating quality, such as states of joy and exuberance.

Fascinated by such experiences, worldly people are forever pursuing situations that produce them. For instance, there are those who accumulate wealth and honors and attract a large entourage, who envision the faces of tutelary deities and mumble magic formulas to restrain evil spirits and to alleviate pain and disease. They clutch at unique meditative experiences that give them extrasensory perceptions and the ability to interpret dreams. They develop a radiating power of body, speech, and mind that irresistibly attracts gods, demons, and men. Their charmed followers flood them with offerings of food, wealth, and pleasure, with immeasurable services and honor. Ultimately such delights and pleasures produce enormous pride and arrogance, which hinder the path to liberation. Therefore, they are called demons.

Yet these so-called demons of hedonistic delights are only based on fictitious mental projections. Truly, for whatever may appear and however it may appear, there is really no such thing as a subject that grasps an object: There is neither appearance, nor mind, nor any interaction between the two. Neither the joy or happiness arising in the mind nor the objects that elicit them have any existence in an absolute sense—not even so much as the tip of a hair!

You can see that all this is like an apparition and a dream, so take it to heart. This is merely the foolish mind getting involved with dreamlike and apparitional qualities. Make this your inner experience, and you will be entirely freed from that overexuberance that is actually nothing at all, even though it is objectified by the mind. Have faith in the great, limitless emptiness of everything, and realize fully that all phenomena are illusory and dreamlike. Take dreams and apparitions as your path, and destroy the illusory demons of hedonistic delights. Then you will discover the true significance of life as apparitional and dreamlike.

The fourth group of demons, my child, are those of subjectivity. The roots of all the other demons meet in subjectivity, so it is of the utmost importance to cut this one off at the source.

This subjectivity is also called belief in a self. Belief in a self is the root of all evil, the cause of all erring in the course of your life. As soon as we take as self that which is not self, the mind becomes emotionally unstable. What we call subjectivity means taking whatever arises, be it good or evil, and clinging to it as ultimately real. But both this object (which is drawn into the subjective field) and this subject (which draws the object into the field), together with all the entities of this phenomenal world, within and without, which we take as me and mine, are recognized by those with higher understanding as being nothing at all.

Get rid of all these demons, which prevent you from achieving liberation, all this grasping at manifestations as the truth. When there is no longer a subject running after an experience, either good or bad, and when all fictitious mental judgments of perceiving and desiring dissolve, anything having to do with mental postulates falls away.

Now perhaps you can understand a little about how to destroy this clinging to a self. You must block the unrestricted outpouring of emotions and free yourself from inner and outer attachments. You must clearly recognize that there is no reality in attachment to anything whatsoever. When you stop grasping at phenomena as being ontologically real, you will see that the ultimate nature of truth is as non-existent as the vast and empty sky. Then you will have destroyed the demons of subjectivity, and with them all the demons arising from emotional instability.

Simply stated, if a self exists as real, then demons also exist. If such a self does not exist, then demons are also non-existent. And there can be no obstacles or hindrances for a self that does not exist. Fear does not exist; trembling from head to foot does not exist.

Intrinsic awareness is free from any kind of limitation. By expanding your awareness to all that can be known, you will savor the fruit of liberation from each of the four types of demons.

So now we have finished this enumeration of the four demons and the instructions on how one destroys them and achieves self-liberated freedom. This teaching is just a short, simple outline, but you, Gan, who are like a son to me, and all others who have the good fortune to hear it: Let it penetrate your mind! Quickly and diligently involve yourself in this teaching. Let it bring forth in you a receptive attitude, and expand your awareness for the well-being of others. That is what I have to say.

A Look into the Skylike Mirror

Lama Mi-pham

*And the whole of the phenomenal world is present
as Dharmakāya's realm.*

A look into the skylike mirror
which is Mind as such,
by which the nature of what is absolute,
in which neither bondage nor freedom exists,
is elucidated.

I bow to the gentle splendor of Samantabhadra,
the self-existing impulse of all life.

This impulse [rig-pa] which has nothing about it
so that it could be found as this or that
is the self-existing pristine cognition
with no periphery or center.

When it is seen in the course of the Guru's instruction
it is the real spontaneous pristine cognition
to which everything points.

This is the real presence of reality, to which everything
    points:
a presence that has nothing of an intellectual creation
    about it.
This is the absolutely real in all reals:
Beyond cause and condition,
it never changes or steps out of itself throughout time.

In this absolute-as-genuineness
that cannot be pointed out by the mind,
all the varied reals are perfect in self-sameness.
The manifestation of its inherent creative motive force
is the appearance of mind with its eight structural
    patterns.
It is in this mind that the multiple manifestations
of samsara and nirvana occur.

The extent of this occurrence is a free occurrence
in and as the ground as pure fact,
and as pure fact it is unconcerned
with profit or harm, acceptance or rejection.
In not knowing the presence of pure fact, but
being taken in by its creative motive force
as an ontological principle,
the notions of subject and object become even more
    hardened.

It is in their range that the variety of
happiness and sorrow, profit and harm is experienced;
though it appears as this variety,
there is nothing in it as such.
It is the power of these fictions of one's own mind
that is of benefit or harm.

Since beginningless time until now
whatever has been experienced
of happiness and sorrow here in samsara
has never been something as such.
It is the empty tricks of one's mind,
the unceasing manifestation nothing but jugglery.

Since the mere fact of mind, indivisibly luminous and open,
is not sullied by any defects or virtues
(as represented by samsara or nirvana),
even if one experiences the torments of the lowest hell,
mind is not in the least hurt by them.

Whatever pleasures may be felt, of and in this world,
they do not change in any way what remains absolute.
The defects and virtues experienced
    as happiness and sorrow
do not cling to it, as little as dye clings to the sky.

Just as when one clings to the color taken on
    by a crystal
as pertaining to the crystal,
so the various displays
of the power of the fictions of the mind,
as well as the various arguments
in the countless philosophical systems,
are set up by the mind.
All the ideas of the intellect
are not what they seem to be;
they fade away in the absolute,
which is not found as a concrete reality.

If one knows what is meant by the absolute, uncreated,
    non-subjective,
it is by knowing one's reality that all reality is free in itself.
The jungle of philosophical systems with their postulates
    of finality
comes to rest in itself,

and the whole of the phenomenal world is present
as Dharmakāya's realm.

Free from all beginning, free as such,
free in its presence, free in its self-sameness,
beyond the postulation of negation and affirmation,
of acceptance and rejection—
the expanding center in which
all the entities of samsara and nirvana
are complete in their self-sameness
by being of the nature of pure fact, actuality, and
    responsiveness—
the one and only creative point,
the meaning of self-existent pristine cognition—
its understanding is said to be the Great Perfection.

This is the goal, the one pursuit, the climax of all pursuits.
Compared with this, all other pursuits, with their acceptance
    and rejections, affirmations and negations,
are called the pursuit of a path
    that is intellectually contrived.
They are all steps toward this one pursuit.

The stages on the path as outlined
    by specific philosophical systems
as well as all the arrangements of the spiritual levels
    and paths,
when they have been ascertained
as the absolute certainty of Buddha awareness,
come to their end effortlessly
in the self-sameness of Reality.

He who runs after the fictions of his own mind
is fettered or freed by the power of these fictions,
but he who knows the absolute
that is without fiction and the same forever,
is one in whom from the beginning
neither bondage nor freedom is observed.

While one will never be satisfied
  with however many pleasures
one may have in this Samsara—
a self-deception by one's own mind,
like the appearances of a dream—
one will also never be weary
even if one experiences hundreds of woes.

Fettered by one's own mind that appears
as this or that without limits,
one roams about incessantly;
but when one understands the meaning of the absolute
where there is neither bondage nor liberation,
one has found the unchanging great bliss.

Instructions on Attaining Inner Calm

Lama Mi-pham

The basis of all good qualities
is the cultivation of your own mind.

I respectfully salute that young being
who possesses the splendor of pure radiance,
who knows both how things really are and how they appear,
whose gentle nature pacifies the waves of mental
    fabrications.
Having done so, I here write this counsel on attaining the
great truth.

Ideas congeal and cloud the stream of consciousness,
which flows uninterruptedly like water.
From beginningless time until today they have accumulated,
but as they are only waves of suffering, lacking in value,

unthinkable, useless, and without certainty,
there is only despair.

These fictional appearances, which arise
within the expanse of all that is, are suffering.
Rooted in these heaps, you cannot obtain
even the slightest good qualities of inner calm and wider
    perspective,
nor the joy of a spontaneous mind. This is the root of
    despair.

Once you know the way to escape
from the noxious habits of mind
by continually inspecting the objective reference
and endeavoring not to waver from that object,
the mind flows together into one-pointedness:
like rolling a scroll.

With all the worldly joys and treasures available to gods
    and men,
control over the mind cannot be attained by fighting.
Rather, it is by letting go of addiction to desired objects,
as a child would let go,
that the mind, naked and quiet, finds joy and delight.

The joy of the ocean of mind when it is untroubled
is like that which comes at the eradication of a plague.
The splendor of unstained bliss like this
is hard to achieve, even if you have some power;
but pushed about by relative forces and phenomena—
    powerless—
Who can experience the bliss of a liberated mind?

Because there is nothing more to experience than this,
Having achieved it, all the splendors and riches
of the world seem like reflected appearances
of the moon and stars in the clear ocean.

Though good things of various kinds—
supernatural powers and the like—may arise,
The basis of all good qualities
is the cultivation of your own mind.
How can good qualities be found in an undisciplined mind?

Therefore, though it is very easy
to waste the life you have in this body,
For the sake of the world cleanse the mind
through the process of continual inspection.
Whatever happens, do not let go.
Wishing and promising thus, do not slacken the effort.

First gradually loosen what is tight,
And by more and more extending the effort,
create the beginning of a habit.
Keeping the mind one-pointedly concentrated
on the object of inspection,
make efforts until that clear, untroubled calm is won.

Having gradually become so accustomed,
examine the acceptance and the rejection,
the good and bad qualities of the mind itself,
making your own thoughts the path.
However long it takes—though months may pass—
continue to make efforts.

A desirous and energetic mind
and the four footholds of practice are the essence.
Surrounded by the chain of inspection,
by the power of steadfastness,
great joy will arise on the mirror of the mind,
filling space to its circumference.

Getting involved with the objective reference
means both examining its pure characteristics
and following the flow of sensations in the body.
Whatever is used as a foundation

(subtle hand-held symbols, letters, or the like),
if you become settled there, success will come.

In this degenerate time, coarse emotions
cloud the mind and the flow of energy.
Like a vicious snake that whirls about, coiling upon itself,
wild fluctuations occur: first restrictions, then the opposite.
The mind becomes very tired of all that,
and immense rejection sets in.

Only by inspecting the nature of mind
while it is in a relaxed and unaffected state,
falling where it wills, can the stream grow steady.
Not following the moving wind of concepts,
knowing the means of leaving them behind,
the expanse of the mind gradually clears,
the jungle of concepts gradually calms—
the ocean of the mind
grows untroubled, radiant, and clean.

This is the foundation of all good qualities,
the unity of inner calm and wider perspective.
By the power of lasting peace, achieved gradually by
    being steadfast,
You come to wider perspective,
the expansive field of intrinsic awareness.
Having labored on the path of great joy and noble actions,
You achieve that range of good qualities—
the unity of inner peace and wider perspective.

The meaning of intrinsic awareness is radiance,
pure from the beginning.
By understanding that within your own mind,
And by inspecting continuously the objective reference
The flow of consciousness is steadied.
This is the gift of all instructions on achieving calm.

Having become settled, the dynamic creativity
    of bliss, clarity,

and freedom from fictional postulates arises in various ways,
and as you approach the primordial experience of being,
it is easy to understand.
Nowadays, this is the usual way to meditate.

But even though you understand the nature of awareness,
if you have not grown accustomed to that reach and range,
pure visions will not appear.
The practices will leave no impression,
and your experience will be like that of ordinary people.
This is not meditation and the Buddha has not taught so.

On the other hand, if you do not understand the nature
    of awareness,
but have only settled into a state of inner peace,
although concepts may be cut off
and some good qualities may manifest,
you do not know the main point—
the freedom that comes from allowing concepts
to remain in their own place.
Still grasping, still bound, you only achieve
the root of samsara—acceptance and rejection.

Therefore you must both understand your own nature
and become firmly settled.
This is the dual foundation
for understanding the mind and for practice.
The meaning of primordial experience
is a field of self-arising radiance.
This is inner peace and wider perspective,
ever spontaneous, ever unified.

These great teachings, explained in hundreds of Sūtras
    and Tantras,
are highly esteemed by everyone.
But just conjuring such things up within your mind is
    not meditation.

Such ordinary activities
do not bring even a little improvement.

It is meaningless, though you look and look at your
    own mind,
if under the power of overexuberant conceptualization
you do not find the knowledge and qualities
    that are possible.
It is like the disturbance of waves in water,
and it produces only greater weariness.

But having begun to follow this primary profound
    instruction,
coming to know everything about taming the helmsman,
    your own mind,
you rest in the happiness of having a great treasure,
and you achieve benefits for both yourself and others.
So quickly strive to realize this!

The great significance of all effort
is only this practice of the cultivation of your own mind.
This good vessel, this treasure of a wish-fulfilling gem,
remains continually in the great and indescribable qualities.

By the good fortune of properly understanding
the significance of this, by remaining devotedly
within this yoga of mind,
freed from all activities, the mind becomes one-pointed.
May all achieve the realization of this very meaningful
    teaching.

For further information on inner calm and its relation to wider perspective, see *Calm and Clear* (Berkeley: Dharma Publishing, 1973) and *Kindly
Bent to Ease Us*, Vol. 1, chapters 10–12 (Berkeley: Dharma Publishing,
1975).

Mind is the Root

Lama Mi-pham

The appearance of a world of objects
is the frolicking of the mind;
if there is no mind, who knows the objects?

Praise to the Jñānasattva Mañjuśrī
who is none other than one's mind,
one with the Guru.

Mind is the root of both samsara and nirvana:
There is no entity of reality that has not sprung from mind.
The frolicking and dancing
of worldly and transworldly apparitions
in all their multiplicity
comes to an end when its creator, mind as magician,
has been overpowered.

Non-understanding is the mind gone astray
into any of the six kinds of existences;
understanding this mind is pristine awareness.

Pristine awareness is Buddhahood, and
as the quintessence of happiness it resides in one's heart.

Hūṁ

Oṁ Āḥ Hūṁ

Look this way: Look at your mind.
Wide are the eyes that look at everything everywhere,
like a beloved child with whom one has long been together.
What is seen compared to what is said to be 'my mind'?
Now is the time to look at this 'my mind'.
Better to take a profound look within
than to let the eyes roam over the external realms.

Even if you were to enter the pristine awareness
in which there is no duality
and which in its intrinsicality has one flavor,
when you have realized that all the entities of reality
are ineffable in being apparitional,
it is by looking at your mind that—in one sweeping
     moment—
you tear open the hidden recesses of the mind
that craves what appears before it
and see the very core of pristine cognitiveness.

Therefore this is called the short cut.
There is no need to unite technique and discrimination
in the unity of the aesthetic continuum
and its intrinsic awareness.
This continuum and its awareness
cannot be added to or abstracted from each other.
This has been laid bare, O fortunate seeker.

A-Ho [Openness and Bliss]

The appearance of a world of objects is the frolicking
     of the mind;
if there is no mind, who knows the objects?
This very act of knowing is not something apart

from the mind.
While there is nothing, there is yet appearance;
this is the self-presentation of the apparitional.

A-Ho

This mind has nothing about it
that could allow it to be taken hold of;
if it had, one could concentrate on what is already there;
if not, one would concentrate on something non-existent.
Do not disrupt unity into such opposites.

A-Ho

That which is not two dispels (the idea of) duality;
that which is not definable as one appears as a duality.
That which cannot be objectified as 'this'
is the self-settledness of the King, Mind-as-such.

A-Ho

Even if one does not know what to concentrate upon,
by seeing it as unattainable
(though not like something thrown away or lost)
you come to the foundations of mind.
Let this attainment be in the realm of the unattainable.
Once you let it be there,
although there is no longer any concrete entity,
you have the creativeness of the all-illumining cognitiveness.
The aesthetic continuum and intrinsic awareness
(which are not two entities)
cannot be added to or subtracted from one another.
In this nothingness they have no essence of nothingness.
If investigated they are nothing as such,
but if left alone they shine in a primal light.
They are not caught by grasping for them,
but are like the moon's reflection in water.

Devoid of any essence such as
cause, effect, presence, or coming-and-going,

the actuality of this openness is a self-existent iridescence.
The response of and to this luminosity never ceases.
How can it be soiled by contradictions and arguments
concerned with non-existence or existence!

In investigating mind, mind is an analogy for pristine
    awareness;
in understanding it, it is the self-present intrinsicality
    in pristine awareness.
What a miracle! This effulgence of mind in Mind-as-such.

What is its use in being open,
what point is there in its appearing?
Who or what is this in which there is no duality?
What is it that is to be concentrated upon?
Preserve it as what it is in its self-settledness.
According to their various capacities,
individuals see this pristine awareness
that is beyond the ordinary mind
gradually or, at best, at once.

In this pristine awareness yogis
burn the seeds of the six kinds of existence—
together with their potentialities—
in the fires of the indestructible nature of reality,
which come as the embodiment, communication, and
    appreciation of values,
that are the self-creativeness
of the pristine awareness in one's heart.

Out of their innermost being the sun of infinite strength and
indestructible confidence shines forth.
Holding this pristine awareness with folded hands,
in a single lifetime they reach primordial Buddhahood.

SAMAYA

I wrote these verses
when I was meditating on Heruka

on the 15th day of the 11th month of the iron-horse year
and felt like an old dog whose teeth
and the bone in its mouth had seemed to become one
and suddenly were vomited.
Or like a young man filled with love,
glancing and swaggering around
while meeting with a beautiful girl
adorned in her finery.
The words came genuinely and spontaneously.

གང་ཞིག་སྐྱོང་ཆེན་གྲུས་འདའི་སེམས།

དམིགས་པའི་ཁ་བཙུན་པོ་ལ།

དན་པའི་ཕྱག་པས་དམ་བཅུང་ནས།

ཤེས་རབ་ལྱུགས་ཀྱུས་རིག་དབང་ཕྱུ།

Firmly Tie the Mind

Firmly tie the mind resembling a mad elephant
To the strong pillar of its perceptual content
With the rope of contemplative inspection
And gradually tame it with the hook
of discrimination.

Let the deceptive appearances subside
in the sphere that is wholly positive,
Since all that ceaselessly appears
as manifested creativeness
Out of the unchanging ground of the
absolutely real
Is the indivisibility of the continuum of reality
and its intrinsic awareness.

གཞི་ད་བྲིངས་འགྱུར་བ་མེད་པ་ལས།

རྩལ་སྣང་འགགས་མེད་རྩྱུང་ཆ་ཀུན།

དབྱིངས་དང་རིག་པ་དབྱེར་མེད་པས།

འཁྲུལ་སྣང་ཀུན་བཟང་ཀློང་དུ་ཐིམ།

Prayer to Śākyamuni Buddha

Lama Mi-pham

As you visualize the Buddha in this way,
think, "He is actually here."

It is said in the Samādhirāja-sūtra:

Those who, while walking, sitting, standing, or reclining
keep in mind the Moon of Sages
and envision him always before them
will be released from suffering.

And further:

One whose mind dwells on the vision
of those whose bodies are gold in color,
those most beautiful protectors of the world,
is equal to the Bodhisattvas.

To practice this yoga of mindfulness of the Master of Sages, the one without equal, the Teacher of us all, begin by taking refuge in the Buddha, Dharma, and Sangha and by cultivating love, compassion, joy, and equanimity. Always stay mindful of the ineffable nature of the appearance of all things.

ĀḤ

Unborn openness,
the unrestricted appearance
of dependent arising
inextricably joined:
the way of illusion.

In the space before you,
amidst an ocean of clouds of offerings,
resting on sun and moon,
on jeweled lion's throne,
the incomparable teacher:
Lion of the Śākyas.

Golden in hue,
endowed with perfect form and features,
He wears the three Dharma robes
and sits cross-legged in the diamond pose.

His right hand reaches to the earth;
his left supports an alms bowl filled with nectar,
in the gesture of repose.

Glorious light blazes forth
as if from a mountain of gold.
The realms of space are filled
with this web of radiant wisdom.

Encircling him are the eight Dharma sons,
the Sixteen Arhats,
and oceans of exalted followers.
By simply remembering the Great Being,
embodiment of all refuges,

they strive for supreme bliss—
freedom from the narrowness
of worldliness or quiescence.

As you visualize the Buddha in this way, think, "He is actually here." Restricted by neither time nor place, the Buddhas, embodiments of wisdom, truly abide within the visualized image. It is said in the Sūtras: "The Buddha dwells in front of all those who set their minds on him; the Buddha always blesses and frees them from faults."

Through visualizing the conqueror, the roots of virtue become inexhaustible. "The one who sees and hears the conqueror gains an immeasurable stock of merit. All the suffering of samsara and all agitation are left behind, and what has been gained is neither lost nor consumed." Establish wishing prayers in the presence of the Conqueror, for the Sūtras teach that prayers so established will bear fruit:

With great compassion
you have embraced this impure, troublesome realm.
Having established five hundred wishing prayers,
you are like the white lotus:
Though you hear great praise, you do not turn back.
I bow to the Compassionate Teacher!

I and others
offer all the pleasures and virtues
of body, speech, and mind,
imagining them as clouds
of wholly good offerings.

With fierce and heartfelt regret,
we confess every wrongful act
accrued from beginningless time.
We rejoice in the virtue of exalted beings:
virtue gathered in the past, present, and future.
May the Wheel of Dharma,

vast and profound, turn without ceasing
in all directions.

Your body of wisdom, like the sky,
dwells unchanging in the three times.
Yet for those who must be trained,
you exhibit the way of birth and death,
your body of magical form forever appearing.

In order to benefit all beings to the ends of space,
having accumulated virtue throughout all times,
may I attain the stage of Conqueror, Lord of Dharma,
always delighting the Dharma kings.

With great mercy you have embraced
all beings of these troubled times,
who are without protection.
Your vast compassion manifests in your work,
whatever form you take throughout time and space.

Pray hold us joyfully in your enlightened compassion,
never forgetting your previous vows.
In heartfelt prayer, with steady faith,
we call upon you,
sole and unequalled refuge.

Tadyathā Oṁ Mune Mune Mahā Mune Śākyamune Ye Svāha

As you repeat this mantra, remember the excellent qualities of the Teacher. With fierce faith and firm mind, one-pointedly visualize his radiant form. As you recite his mantra and express his qualities, there appear from the body of the Teacher innumerable wisdom rays extending to all living beings, clearing away obscurations. Imagine that you and all these beings are on the excellent Mahāyāna path, and that you have reached the stage from which you will not fall back to samsara. Make efforts in this way, as much as possible.

Vajra Guru Mantra

. . . O Guru, if one should rely solely on your sādhana which is the Vajra Guru Mantra, what benefit and advantage will come from this?

The Buddhism of Tibet is remarkable for the great variety of practices it offers to those who elect to travel the path to liberation from the sufferings of human existence. Among these various practices the use of mantra forms an important part, so much so that the Tibetan form of Buddhism is often referred to as Mantrayāna, the Mantra Vehicle.

Properly used, under competent guidance, mantra is an effective instrument for dispelling the ignorance on which our anxious lives are founded. It can lead the practitioner to a realization of the true nature of mind. For mantra is not a form of magical incantation, but rather a scientific method for bringing the mind into harmony with subtle levels of awareness and reopening avenues of communication that otherwise remain closed.

The Vajra Guru Mantra is the mantra of Guru Padma-sambhava, the founder of Buddhism in Tibet. It is said to be especially beneficial for these troubled times, for it has great power to calm the tensions and anxieties so common to our age. If one sits quietly and concentrates complete attention upon one's own voice chanting the mantra, the worry and distress that continuously keep the mind in turmoil will gradually subside, and the mind will slowly be suffused with a deep calm.

With practice, it is possible to extend the period of peaceful concentration, thus creating a refuge from fears, doubts, and other painful mental distractions. As this serenity develops and expands, the mind gradually settles, like the surface of a still pool. From this calm, awareness arises, so that the self-nature of mind can be realized.

To traverse the path, an element of faith is required. This is not a blind, uncritical acceptance, but an openness: a willingness to search and to discover for oneself the wisdom which has been maintained and transmitted by a continuous tradition extending back thousands of years.

Buddhism has always maintained that for those who seek within themselves, critically, persistently, and with intensity, the truth of the Dharma is self-evident. The path that leads to realization is thus a path of examination. This is true for the practice of mantra as well. The power of mantra will be revealed to those who follow the time-honored teachings with patience, sincerity, and trust.

Excerpt of an Adaptation from the Tibetan

Herein is Contained
The Commentary on the Mystic Syllables and the Benefits
of the Vajra Guru Mantra
from the gTer-ma of sPrul-sku Karma Gling-pa

A na dza sha ma wa zha ma rga rma
Vajra Guru Deva Ḍākinī Hūṁ

Homage to the Lama, the Yidam, and the Ḍākinī

The Ḍākinī Ye-shes-mtsho-rgyal spoke:

I, Ye-shes-mtsho-rgyal, who am a mere woman, having
made an offering of a vast mandala, outer, inner, and secret,
to my Guru, now make this request. O Master Padmasambhava, please grant to us, we who are the people of
Tibet, your unending aid and assistance in this present life
and in all future lives. There has never been before, nor will
there in the future ever come forth again a boon as great as
yourself. I have no doubt that even I, who am a mere woman,
shall be given your sādhana, which is itself like a pure and
precious nectar.

I see that there will come a time in the distant future
when human beings will possess fickle intellects and ever-
changing opinions. They will be very excitable, impatient,
and excessively prone to violence. They will cling to false
views regarding the holy Dharma. In particular, they will
slander and belittle the doctrine of the supremely secret
mantras. At that time, for all sentient beings the three great
evils of disease, poverty, and warfare with terrifying weapons
will greatly increase. In particular, there will come a time of
terrible suffering for Tibet and the Tibetan people. Just as
ants swarm out of their nest when the nest is broken open,
so troubles will swarm with great devastation across the
three regions of China, Tibet, and Central Asia.

Ye-shes-mtsho-rgyal, the Tibetan queen who became one of Padmasambhava's foremost disciples.

O Guru, you have proclaimed many skillful means for curing these ills. But for the people of those future times there will be no time or opportunity for the practice of sādhana. Only a very few will even have the desire to practice. On every hand disturbances and distractions will be exceedingly strong and powerful. Human beings will be unable to agree among themselves. Even the materials necessary for pūjā and the preparation for sādhana practice will be incomplete.

In such evil times, it will be extremely difficult to avert or reverse those trends. In such times as those, O Guru, if one should rely solely on your sādhana which is the Vajra Guru Mantra, what benefit and advantage will come from this? For the sake of those future beings with inferior intellects, devoid of deep spiritual understanding, please tell us.

Then the Great Master spoke:

O faithful daughter, what you have said is very true. But in such future periods of time as those, it is still certain that from practice there shall come forth benefits both immediate and ultimate for all sentient beings. I shall conceal the eighteen kinds of gTer-mas, such as earth-treasures, water-treasures, rock-treasures, and sky-treasures, which will contain countless numbers of sādhanas and secret teachings.

In those evil times, the skillful methods of those who possess good karma and the auspicious coinciding of circumstances will be exceedingly difficult to accomplish. Such times are characterized by the exhaustion of whatever merit sentient beings may possess.

Nevertheless, if at such places as the twenty-four Great Places of Pilgrimage, or in the temples and villages, or on the peak of a great mountain, or on the shore of a great river, or in the uplands and lowlands inhabited by gods, demons, and ghosts, if there is one who possesses the vows of the Sangha, or even a layman of devout faith or a woman of good character, having intensively cultivated the intention to attain enlightenment, who is able to repeat the essence of the Vajra Guru Mantra one hundred times or one thousand or ten thousand or one hundred thousand or one million or one hundred million times or as many times as possible, the resulting power and benefits will be inconceivable to the human mind.

And in all the directions of space, the evils of disease, poverty, warfare, hostile armies, civil strife, famine, dire prophecies, and ill omens shall be averted. In every direction, the good fortune of healthy cattle, abundant crops and rain in season shall come. In one's present life, in all future lives, and in the narrow, difficult passage of the bar-do, I shall speak to the superior person in his dreams. And it is certain that such a person, having perfected gradually the paths and the stages, shall enter into the land of Camaradvīpa as a Vidyādhara, whether male or female.

If one but repeats the mantra uninterruptedly one hundred times a day, he will appear in the thoughts of others in favorable fashion. There will come to him effortlessly abundant food, wealth, and good fortune. If one repeats the mantra as often as one thousand times or ten thousand times and so on, he shall gain control over the minds of others, and it is certain that he shall attain power and blessing.

If one repeats the mantra one hundred thousand or ten million times or more, he will accumulate all the power of the three worlds and gain control over the three realms of existence. Gods and demons shall become his servants, and he shall attain without any impediment whatsoever the Four Magical Rites. Then he will be able to help immeasurably all sentient beings as much as he desires. If one is able to count as many as thirty million or seventy million, then all the Buddhas of the three times of past, present, and future shall always be with him. Indeed, he shall be identical with me. All the gods, rakṣasas, and fierce mountain deities shall promise to listen to his commands and obey him, accomplishing whatever he entrusts to them.

The superior person will in this very life attain the rainbow body. The intermediate person will on the occasion of the 'Chi-kha'i bar-do realize the clear light of self-illumination ('od-gsal). Even the inferior person, once having seen my face in the bardo, will be delivered from the arising of the (expected) appearances, and having been reborn in Camaradvīpa, he shall give immeasurable aid to all sentient beings.

Then the Ḍākinī Ye-shes-mtsho-rgyal further requested:

O Great Master, we thank you for such a great boon of vast and immeasurable power and benefit. But for the sake of future sentient beings, please expound briefly in sūtra fashion on the immeasurable power and benefit of the commentary on the mystic syllables of the Mantra of Guru Padma.

Then the Great Master spoke:

O daughter of a noble family, that which is called the Vajra Guru Mantra is not only my name, but represents the very heart of vital essence of the Yidams, the four types of Tantras, the Nine Vehicles, and the eighty-four thousand sections of the Dharma. This Mantra is complete and perfect, for it is the very essence of all the Buddhas of the three times, of all the Gurus, Devatas, Dākinīs, and Dharmapālas.

If one should ask what marks the cause of this perfection, then let him listen well and fix it firmly in his mind. Let him repeat the mantra again and again. Let him write it down. Then let him instruct and explain its meaning to all sentient beings of future ages.

OṀ ĀḤ HŪṀ
VAJRA GURU PADMA SIDDHI HŪṀ

As for Oṁ, Āḥ, and Hūṁ, they are the supreme essence of the Body, Speech, and Mind. Vajra is the supreme essence of the Vajra family. Guru is the supreme essence of the Ratna family. Padma is the supreme essence of the Padma family. Siddhi is the supreme essence of the Karma family. As for Hūṁ, it is the supreme essence of the Tathāgata family.

OṀ ĀḤ HŪṀ
VAJRA GURU PADMA SIDDHI HŪṀ

As for Oṁ, it is the perfection of the Sambhogakāya, which embodies the Buddhas of the Five Families. Āḥ is the perfection complete and unchanging of the Dharmakāya. Hūṁ is the perfection of the Guru, who is the Nirmāṇakāya, in the space before one. Vajra is the perfection of the divine assembly of Herukas. Guru is the perfection of the divine assembly of Guru Vidyādharas. Padma is the perfection of the divine assembly of Ḍakas and Ḍākiṇīs. Siddhi is the vital energy of all the Wealth Gods and Treasure Lords. Hūṁ is the vital energy of all the Dharmapālas, without exception.

OṀ ĀḤ HŪṀ
VAJRA GURU PADMA SIDDHI HŪṀ

As for Oṁ, Āḥ, and Hūṁ, they are the vital energies of the three types of Tantras (Father, Mother, and Nondual). Vajra is the vital energy of the two sections called the Vinaya and the Sūtras. Guru is the vital energy of the sections Abhidharma and Kriyātantra. Padma is the vital energy of the two called Upāya Tantra and Yoga Tantra. Siddhi is the vital energy of the two called Mahāyoga and Anuyoga. Hūṁ is the vital energy of the Atiyoga.

OṀ ĀḤ HŪṀ
VAJRA GURU PADMA SIDDHI HŪṀ

By Oṁ, Āḥ, and Hūṁ, all obscurations that derive from the three poisons will be purified. By Vajra all obscurations that derive from hatred will be purified. By Guru all obscurations that derive from pride will be purified. By Padma all obscurations that derive from greed will be purified. By Siddhi all obscurations that derive from envy will be purified. By Hūṁ all obscurations that derive from all forms of emotionality will be purified.

OṀ ĀḤ HŪṀ
VAJRA GURU PADMA SIDDHI HŪṀ

By Oṁ, Āḥ, and Hūṁ one will obtain the Dharmakāya, Sambhogakāya, and Nirmāṇakāya. By Vajra one will obtain the Mirror-like Wisdom. By Guru one will obtain the Wisdom of Sameness. By Padma one will obtain the Discriminating Wisdom. By Siddhi one will obtain the All-Accomplishing Wisdom. By Hūṁ one will perfectly obtain all that derives from Wisdom.

OṀ ĀḤ HŪṀ
VAJRA GURU PADMA SIDDHI HŪṀ

By Oṁ, Āḥ, and Hūṁ, one will control gods, demons, and men. By Vajra one will control such hostile spirits as gandharvas and fire spirits. By Guru one will control such hostile spirits as Yama and the rakṣasas. By Padma one will control such hostile spirits as water sprites and air spirits. By Siddhi one will control such hostile spirits as yakṣas and powerful demons. By Hūṁ one will control such hostile spirits as planetary genii and earth lords.

OṀ ĀḤ HŪṀ
VAJRA GURU PADMA SIDDHI HŪṀ

By Oṁ, Āḥ, and Hūṁ one will obtain the six perfections. By Vajra one will realize all the magical rites that are peaceful. By Guru one will realize all the magical rites that increase prosperity. By Padma one will realize all the magical rites of overpowering enchantment. By Siddhi one will realize all the magical rites of worldly success. By Hūṁ one will realize all the magical rites that are terrifying.

OṀ ĀḤ HŪṀ
VAJRA GURU PADMA SIDDHI HŪṀ

By Oṁ, Āḥ, and Hūṁ one will counteract the magical influences of both Lamas and Bonpos. By Vajra one will counteract the hostile influences of the nemesis of the gods. By Guru one will counteract the hostile influences of gods, rakṣasas, and nature deities. By Padma one will counteract the hostile influences of minor worldly deities and demons. By Siddhi one will counteract the hostile influences of Nāgas and earth-lords. By Hūṁ one will counteract all the hostile influences of gods, demons, and men.

OṀ ĀḤ HŪṀ
VAJRA GURU PADMA SIDDHI HŪṀ

By Oṁ, Āḥ, and Hūṁ one will vanquish the militant hosts of the five poisons. Vajra will vanquish the militant hosts born of hatred. Guru will vanquish the militant hosts born of pride. Padma will vanquish the militant hosts born of greed. Siddhi will vanquish the militant hosts born of envy. By Hūṁ one will vanquish the militant hosts of gods, demons, and men.

OṀ ĀḤ HŪṀ
VAJRA GURU PADMA SIDDHI HŪṀ

By Oṁ, Āḥ, and Hūṁ one will obtain the siddhis of body, speech, and mind. By Vajra one will obtain the siddhis of the peaceful and wrathful deities. By Guru one will obtain the siddhis of the Vidyādhara Guru. By Padma one will obtain the siddhis of the Ḍākinīs and Dharmapālas. By Siddhi one will obtain siddhis both ordinary and supreme. By Hūṁ one will obtain all conceivable siddhis.

OṀ ĀḤ HŪṀ
VAJRA GURU PADMA SIDDHI HŪṀ

By Oṁ, Āḥ, and Hūṁ one will be reborn in the Primordial realm. By Vajra one will be reborn in the Realm of Manifest Happiness, in the eastern direction. By Guru one will be reborn in the Fortunate Realm, in the southern direction. By Padma one will be reborn in the Realm of Great Bliss, in the western direction. By Siddhi one will be reborn in the Realm of Infinite Peace, in the northern direction. By Hūṁ one will be reborn in the Realm of Emptiness, in the center.

How to Practice the Teachings

dPal-sprul Rinpoche

Practice today:
Travel the path to liberation!

It is said in the Sūtras:

Worthy son, think of yourself as a patient,
think of the teachings as medicine;
think of the spiritual guide as a wise physician;
think of earnest practice as the cure.

Suppose you are stricken by a severe illness. You go at once to a skilled physician. Following the doctor's orders, you carefully take the medicine he prescribes, directing all your energy toward gaining relief from your sickness.

This selection was adapted from the first chapter of the Kun-bzang-bla-ma'i-zhal-lung.

Now, the self is like an invalid. From time without beginning, it has circled about in a great ocean of suffering, tormented by the misery caused by the poisons of desire, hatred, and ignorance. The teacher is the skilled physician. To find release from the illness of suffering, emotionality, and karma, you must take the medicine of the excellent teaching, and then act on what is taught.

Even if you rely on a teacher, if you do not practice according to his instructions, you are like the patient who does not listen to the doctor's advice and therefore cannot be helped. If you do not take as practice the medicine of the excellent teaching, you are like the sick person who leaves countless prescriptions lying unused by his pillow; he will not be cured.

Today there are some people who go to teachers and with great feeling cry out to them, "Gaze upon me with your great compassion!" But all the while they continue to amass unwholesome actions. They think that the teacher's compassion will pick them up and fling them like a stone into the pure realms. They think that they can escape the results of their actions. But being taken under the wing of the teacher's compassion means that the teacher, out of great kindness, takes an interest in you. He teaches you the profound precepts. He sets forth what is to be taken up and what is to be put aside. He teaches the path of liberation according to the Conqueror's word. What is more compassionate than this? Now, having met with such compassion, whether you travel the path of liberation depends solely on you.

Keep in mind that you have obtained a fortunate human existence. You know the essentials of what is to be done. You have the ability to act. This very moment is the boundary between abiding happiness and abiding misfortune. So once you have taken up practice in accordance with the teacher's instructions, it is important to come to a final decision about samsara and nirvana.

At the time when the monks gather around your dead body, the border between going up to fortunate states of existence and going down to the lower realms is crossed as easily as a horse is led by the bit. If you have not practiced the path, at that time you are driven from behind by the fierce red wind of karma and welcomed in front by the black obscurity of fear. Squeezed into the long, narrow passage of the intermediate state, you find yourself face to face with the unthinkable Lord of Death, who pursues you with shouts of "Strike! Strike! Kill! Kill! Every place of escape or hiding, every refuge and hope is gone. In this state of complete terror will come the border between going up and going down.

The great teacher from O-rgyan has said:

When initiation is bestowed
on the figure of the deceased,
it is already too late.
His consciousness is already roving
like a mad dog in the intermediate state.
Remembering better states of existence,
he has a very difficult time.

Truly the border is crossed as easily as a horse is led by the bit. But this border is here *now*, in this very condition of being alive!

Accomplishing an upward, wholesome action now, when you have a human body, has greater power than doing such an action while in other states of being. But you also have a greater capacity now to accumulate unwholesome, downward actions. Doing so will surely cause bondage in the depth of the worst existences. So do not forfeit your human skull.

Having met the teacher, who is like a learned doctor, and the excellent teachings, which are like a nectar that heals even death, practice the teachings that you hear. Practice today: Travel the path to liberation!

One Moon

dPal-sprul Rinpoche

In order to benefit beings,
one lama seems to come and go.

Introduction

The guide who safely leads us through dangerous or un-
known territory is a valued companion. How much more
valued is the guide who leads us from the dark forest of
ignorance and unhappiness into the light of full understanding. In Tibetan Buddhism, this guide is called the lama. The
term means 'higher one'; it refers both to respected religious
teachers and to the spark of inner intelligence and knowledge within each of us.

In this selection, drawn from the Chos-dang-'jigs-rten
shes-pa'i bstan-bcos-gdol-ba'i drang-srong-gi gtam-thar-pa'i
them-skas (A Ladder to Liberation), dPal-sprul Rinpoche
uses the images of the moon changing through time and
circumstance to illustrate how our attitude toward the lama

is colored by judgments and capacity. This fluctuating and subjective view becomes a metaphor, inviting us to perceive all 'things' and events with a more open and expansive mind, free from judgments and emotionality, aware of deep meaning in all that one does and is, in touch with the awakened quality at the very core of being.

By the power of circumstance,
one moon appears through time as large or small.
By the power of needs,
one lama arises in different disguises.

By the power of vessels of water,
one moon appears in myriad reflections.
By the power of minds,
one lama appears as many.

By the power of clouds,
one moon is bright or dark.
By the power of concepts,
one lama appears as good or bad.

By the power of karma,
one moon seems to comfort or menace.
By the power of thought,
one lama arouses faith or disdain.

By the power of day or night,
one moon rises and sets.
In order to benefit beings,
one lama seems to come and go.

dPal-sprul Rinpoche's Counsels

*In brief, the central point
is that you must remain
truly aware of yourself at all times.*

Three things must not be forgotten:
the grace-filled Guru,
the compassion-filled Buddha,
mindfulness of your instructions.

Three things must be remembered:
the root-guru who initiates,
the message he teaches,
the vows you take.

Three things must stay in their proper place:
mind with body,
body on your cushion,
mind in relaxation.

Three things are best forgotten:
anger at enemies,
desire for objects,
drowsy inattentiveness.

Three rules should be held:
no public oration,
privately keep hands quiet,
mindful at all times.

Three things should be kept secret:
your knowledge,
others' faults,
future plans.

Three things should not be made a display:
transient enthusiasm,
ruses and pretensions,
specific practices.

Three things should be avoided:
squabbles,
crowds,
gambling dens.

Three things should not be discussed:
false teachings,
private matters with strangers,
impossible marvels.

Three things should not be held:
inconstant feelings toward friends,
inconstant speech,
inconstant action.

Three things should not be displayed:
prideful show,
backbiting,
any snobbishness.

Three things should not be done:
bootlicking,
heeding false teachers,
revealing secrets.

Three things should not be neurotically dwelt upon:
beautiful women's bodies,
friends' actions,
your own good qualities.

Three things should be followed:
diplomatic speech with friends,
local customs,
Dharma by the mind.

Three things should not be heeded:
flattery,
hasty reactions,
a shallow brain's instructions.

Three things should not be coveted:
riches of wealthy men,
insignia of high office,
priceless ornamentation.

Three persons should not be disparaged:
respected persons,
business competitors,
admirers.

Three persons should not be praised:
unpopular persons,
egotists,
your own child, to others.

Three persons should not be disparaged or praised:
relatives,
teachers not known to you,
actually, anyone at all.

And so forth . . .

In brief, the central point
is that you must remain
truly aware of yourself at all times.
Such is the sacred and the secular.
In a word: This is the teaching.

Ritual Practice: Entering the Mandala

Tarthang Tulku

To see something in its mandala form is to be drawn to its center.

The Vajrayāna is a science of human being, a rigorous methodology for arriving at knowledge. Carefully crafted and based on a strong foundation of understanding, its rituals are intended to produce results which are both concrete and profound. For one who wishes to test this claim, the Vajrayāna extends an open invitation: It is only necessary to undergo a thorough preparation—mentally, physically, and emotionally—and then the path is open to experience and the opportunity to determine its value for oneself.

Those who are opposed to ritual tend to dismiss it on two opposing grounds. For some, it is too other-worldly: unrealistic or even escapist. For others, already committed to a meditative practice, it is too worldly: a childish prop or crutch that detracts from the true mystic experience and indicates a low level of spiritual attainment. But the ceremonies of the Vajrayāna fall into neither of these two extremes. Vigorous and eminently practical, they aim at specific goals that have as their direct consequence compassionate and effective action in the world. Formless meditation is well known in Vajrayāna practice, as is the call for action that benefits others. If ritual sādhanas, whose performance requires unparalleled mastery of meditative skills, had no special virtue or advantage of their own, the Vajrayāna would not bother to employ them.

Vajrayāna sādhanas are intended to remedy human alienation from the totality of what is: the energies that constitute the play of the universe, and their corresponding active presence within the human microcosm. Thus, sādhanas are performed at times when interplay between human embodiment and the surrounding cosmos is most accessible—times when certain energy configurations allow ready communication between microcosm and macrocosm. Guru Padmasambhava promised that he would come to those performing his sādhana on certain days of the lunar month. At such times, the interplay of inner and outer reveals the connection between the human and what is often called the divine. Through rightly directed action, this harmony can be nurtured into a virtual unity.

While based on the teachings of the Mahāyāna regarding the true nature of samsara and nirvana, the Vajrayāna gives these teachings precise content and offers the skillful means needed to act according to this knowledge. Ritual sādhana makes it possible to master the interplay of form and formlessness, action and wisdom. Through mastery of the psychic energies of the body and the range of meditative practice, the truth of 'emptiness' is transformed from a noble ideal into a concrete and dynamic reality. The six perfections are no longer an externally imposed moral code but an integral aspect of reality. Generating bodhicitta becomes a yogic practice for transforming the nature of mind in this moment. The confession of faults expresses the realization that past, present, and future—the field for the play of karma—are immediately accessible now, so that past karmic defilements can be freely transmuted. Taking refuge takes on esoteric significance, as the object of this practice is ultimately experienced as being identical with ourselves. The traditional dedication of merit becomes more than a pious wish—the joy of realization, expressed through the sādhana, becomes the vehicle for acting effectively on behalf of all sentient beings. Sādhana forms a bridge through which the vows and intention of the Bodhisattva are fully and realistically integrated with every motion and expression, however simple or mundane. The very essence of the Buddha's teachings, the pulse and flow of reality, are to be found within the mandalas of the Vajrayāna sādhana.

In performing a sādhana, the practitioner enters a sacred mandala, which may be understood as a form consisting of a center and its radiating emanations. Together, center and periphery express the truth of what is and the way or ways in which it reveals itself. What surrounds and emerges from the center is understood to share in its intrinsic beauty. To contemplate these emanations offers a way of understanding the point at the center. At the same time, by seeing these emanations as just that—as nothing over and above what is found at the center—one appreciates them as 'nothing special', at once 'empty' and 'divine'. Through participating in the mandala, we learn to welcome the phenomena of our world, rather than taking them for granted, shunning them, or greedily grasping for them. In this way, we ourselves become the center of the mandala.

To enter the mandala, we must be ready to accept our own being as it actually is (instead of as we might like or imagine ourselves to be). Whether we enter the mandala physically or in visualization, we bring with us all that we are: Thoughts, feelings, perceptions are all fully there and actively engaged. There is nothing 'private' to hold back or keep dormant. Past actions, experience, devotion, attainments, and karmic patterns join with future hopes and fears. The unfolding ritual of the sādhana turns everything to its purpose. The common elements of our lives are not abandoned; instead our notions and evaluations about them are surrendered, so that we can 're-cognize'. In this way we can be born anew into the world.

This process of reintegration happens when we see our own being and all the constituents of our experience as mandalas in their own right, finding their place in the larger mandala. Each sense faculty and all of them together, each sense object and all of them collectively, as well as the interaction of the senses and their objects—all these are understood to partake of the mandala character. As the chakras interact, the five skandhas become the five wisdoms. To understand this—through performance of the sādhana—does not mean a reconstruction of reality, nor a projection onto reality. Rather, it is the realization of what is and always has been the case.

To see something in its mandala form is to be drawn to its center. Here, at the center, is where Guru Rinpoche resides in one of his many aspects. In being led to him and to this insight, we are led back to ourselves. And in understanding ourselves, we understand everyone else. The natural expression of this understanding is action.

To assist in achieving this sublime purpose, the sādhanas of the Vajrayāna are rich in sights and sounds. Traditional practice calls for simultaneously reciting texts, chanting mantra, visualizing, and practicing 'form' and 'formless' meditations. Each of these practices has an open-ended content whose effect and significance changes and deepens with practice. The texts and practices evoke meaning and call forth energies on the level of practice, insight, devotion, meditative attainments, tradition, and the application of remedies to overcome obstacles. When wisdom is activated, these various aspects and practices do not remain separate and isolated; since their nature is śūnyatā, the difference and boundaries tend to dissolve. This is why Vajrayāna practices are not props and do not require a neurotic clinging to a constructed 'emptiness'. The energies of all the sādhana practices converge, producing one-pointedness.

Through the practice of sādhana, an all-embracing yet subtle transformation occurs. One's own efforts become inseparable from the practice of accumulating merit (puṇya sambhara) and skillful action on behalf of others. This union is given specific form by the central figure of the mandala, from which it emanates. At the same time, insight into emptiness reveals that there is nothing to be transmuted—no one acting and no action. Realization is also empty, and there is nothing to attain. While on one level we seek to purify and consecrate ourselves and our world, on another level we understand that there has never been a departure from purity. Coincident with a ritual emphasis on external beauty is an appreciation that such beauty simply mirrors and points to the intrinsic beauty of everything.

Yet this experience, transcendent and complete in itself, is neither inactive nor unresponsive. It is luminescent, not limited in its scope by being a 'possession' of the meditator. The joy of aesthetic appreciation does not depend on making the split into subject and object, and so it can never become simply an ecstatic stupor. Such bliss or ecstasy is not the subjective experience of a swollen or intoxicated ego but a central feature of reality. Indeed, the sādhana's influence depends on a continuous flow and interchange: There is no experience to be stopped or dammed up by the self. Within the mandala, one is a 'center' without being a 'center of gravity'.

This unlimited truth, which is also unlimited beauty and unlimited ecstasy, is the expression of the limitless understanding of śūnyatā. There is nothing 'there' to block our awareness and comprehension, nothing to serve as a basis for grasping, selfishness, or delusion. On this basis, complete and effective dedication of merit becomes natural, for there are no boundaries or barriers to overcome. The way of being that has been activated is inherently radiant, not limited by the restrictions of a self-conscious understanding.

This shift, which is at the heart of sādhana practice, is a move from the limitless, unformed 'truth' of Dharmakāya to the 'body' of the Sambhogakāya: reality in its presentation and operation as spontaneous communication and responsiveness. With the Sambhogakāya, all isolation, barriers, and distance between ourselves and others simply vanishes.

It is from the Sambhogakāya that the sādhana derives its power, and its practices, taken singly and together, all express the Sambhogakāya dynamic. In entering the mandala, we expose ourselves to the Sambhogakāya influence. Perhaps at first we are not aware of this, but still we are touched at some deep level, and can open ourselves more, becoming more receptive. The Sambhogakāya stimulates and awakens each person in the most appropriate way, encouraging a reciprocal and empathetic response to the energies of the sādhana. The more we respond, the more open to this influence we become, making possible a still greater and more appreciative engagement and sensitivity. Increasing knowledge, together with the accumulated power traditionally transmitted through initiations, enhance sensitivity to what is happening and intensify the capacity to participate.

At a certain point this cyclical process may mount to a point of breakthrough, making it possible to realize the goal of Sambhogakāya action. Though the path to this point can be a long one, there need be no cause for fear or concern. Whatever the motive with which one begins to practice, the path itself never departs from this genuine mode of being, (which is also a being-for-others); there is little danger of going astray.

The Vajrayāna proceeds from a twofold recognition. On the one hand, human beings feel estranged from reality and desire deliverance from the sorrow that this estrangement brings. On the other hand, this feeling of estrangement, together with the process through which deliverance takes place, are only part of reality's play.

Vajrayāna sādhanas incorporate the kinds of action and self-expression that are appropriate to each of these points of view. Human beings are supplicants and also wholly fulfilled, and in both these modes of being they take their place within the mandala. Every sādhana concludes by affirming their identity. The natural response, spontaneously generated, is one of reverence and joyous celebration.

Part Three

Teachings
for the West

An Interview
with Tarthang Tulku

American young people have a true heart. There is sincerity, and there is much interest in truth and spiritual life.

Crystal Mirror: As a Tibetan lama, one of the first teachers of Tibetan Buddhist practice in America, a husband and father, an advisor and friend for a number of people, you have many difficulties and many responsibilities to meet, from the spiritual to the financial. Could you describe what a typical day is like for you?

Rinpoche: Well . . . We get up at about 6 o'clock, and practice for the house starts at 6:30. We practice prostrations, and at the same time do chanting. Also, we do silent meditation. Then we go to breakfast. After breakfast each individual has various jobs and practices. I meet with maybe four or five students every morning, up to 8:30. Then I go

---

This interview was conducted in 1972.

upstairs and maybe talk with my family. I sometimes read or rest about half an hour. I come back down about 10 o'clock and sometimes go to the library or see to the office, books, and records, answer letters. . . then lunch.

Sometimes visitors from far away come unexpectedly, or some days we have ritual ceremonies. On weekends are the practice classes or seminars. And usually each day there are emotional problems and business, financial problems, and I need to talk to many people plus family activities, and then . . . (laughing) children. Sometimes it's physically exhausting. So I don't need to leave the Center very often because my job is mostly here. Does that answer your question?

Crystal Mirror: Yes. Is there anything that you have been wanting to do since you came here that you haven't had time for so far?

Rinpoche: Not much. I haven't had much vacation, but I don't think that's too important. I know about vacation and that kind of activity. When I am on vacation I like it very much, but I also know the end result before I go. After vacation, a month later, the pleasure is gone, the happiness is just gone. But if I recognize this before I go, why should I spend this time? Better to do something—to all the time fight. That's like . . . (laughing) . . .

Crystal Mirror: Are you satisfied with the progress you and the Meditation Center have made here—are your efforts having the result you hoped for?

Rinpoche: Yes, I think progress is quite good. Of course, there are many problems and obstacles . . . People have many doubts and dissatisfactions that I must deal with. And that's very difficult, because the attitudes and concepts here are not the same as what I grew up with. Before I can help someone, he must express his problem precisely—then I can do something, can draw a very clear picture of the situation. But this takes lots of time and talking, and there are language difficulties. There are many emotional and personality problems, and when these are settled, there are always others—financial and house problems, sickness, always something. This is a pretty big job. We have sixty people here, and there's much to do. Sometimes I get physically and emotionally tired, but if I rest and eat well, then I am strong again.

It's all right, you know, because whatever efforts I make now should all be for Dharma. I didn't do as much with my Gurus as I had wished to—now, if I can't continue my own studies then it is best that whatever merit my body, my spirit, my life may have be dedicated to the Dharma. If I can help people a little then I am happy, because I realize that fortune, name, and material success are not very important.

I've seen many sides of these. My family and all my relatives in Tibet were wealthy and prominent people, and my father was a very famous lama. One other lama and I shared all the responsibilities of my monastery. Then I left my home to study in Khams for six or seven years—most of my Gurus were there—and I became separated from all these things. They all became quite dream-like. During the time I was studying, some of my Gurus were very wrathful men—their training was extremely strict. Food was scarce. I was often very hungry and alone in frightening places. I met many different kinds of people—sometimes they were very kind and helpful, sometimes they were bandits who took everything away. Sometimes I had servants to help me, sometimes I was alone or completely unrecognized by everyone.

Then when I left Khams, I traveled great distances on foot and had to deal with many officials in various places. And after being alone for so long, suddenly all the Tibetan refugees came. We were practically a whole nation of people together. There were many problems in adjusting to the situation in India, the new language and customs. Then we established ourselves at the university, set up jobs, began publications. We tried to encourage the young lamas. It was a difficult time. People were dying or starving. . . . Some were very disturbed because they had lost their family and country and fortune—they had been through many disasters.

So I stayed in India for about ten years, and then traveled through Europe, and today I am here. I believe I've had much experience of samsara. So now I am not too materially oriented. I am only interested in helping people as much as I can. This kind of benefit seems more substantial to me, and it gives me the only pleasure I seek.

Crystal Mirror: The use of a wide variety of drugs has already caused many changes in our society. Would you comment on this trend?

Rinpoche: I could make many comments. Even some spiritual people say drugs are wonderful, like a teacher. They say because Westerners are so rationalistic, the only way to approach the Dharma is through some drug like LSD. Well . . . I feel that in following the Dharma, particularly Vajrayāna, the body is very sacred, speech is very sacred, and the mind is very sacred—like three jewels, even though we may not recognize it. Chemical reactions make changes. Vajrayāna requires pure nature. So there's no drugs in Vajrayāna.

Many students talk to me and say, "Well, if I hadn't taken LSD, I might not be here." Maybe that's true, maybe true. Anyway, since they joined the Center, if I have the power, I say, don't take drugs.

In some aspects maybe drugs bring a little understanding, more liberal, open, friendly. But those who take drugs, they are . . . I'm sorry . . . they're lost, they're desperate. They cannot take care of themselves; the mind is like "aaahh . . . aaahh . . . ": beaten with all kinds of pressures, and so they cannot survive without drugs. Many young people are lost; they do not have very good friends. Their family does not take care of them, and society doesn't care about them.

Too much individuality, struggles, power, all kinds of problems. They take all kinds of drugs to take this away.

But my advice is, once someone has experience, they now have some realization, and they do not need to keep taking drugs. This is especially true for someone who has some understanding of meditation. If he has faith, that will take care of him. For instance, some of our students took heavy drugs, even heroin, for many years, and now that is finished, and there is no problem. Even Western medicine does not know the way to cure this kind of sickness. So I think having more and more trust in the Dharma is good. . . . That is my comment.

Crystal Mirror: Do you think the prevailing sexual attitudes in this country cause special problems for Dharma study?

Rinpoche: Yes. Sexual problems are very much a problem here, as compared to Tibet. But I think the young people have some sort of understanding, because they have quite a lot of experience.

Sex is mostly a mental problem, not really a physical problem. If you create more images and ideas, that makes more excitement, and then sexual desires are created. If you control your mind and fantasies, not much sexual desire arises.

Something similar happens if you have lots of experience with sex. In some countries there is a very big problem, more than America, because they cannot have sex until the age of twenty-one. Or they cannot have sex till after marriage, but then the marriage is arranged within the families, and you cannot have a marriage based on love. But in America they go here and there, all different times, many changes. They have tasted all kinds. So they do not have much fascination, just asking "How is it?" Someone who has tasted sex is maybe not so fascinated. Sex gets old, and maybe sometimes you're tired of it.

Crystal Mirror: Do people ever think you're a demigod?

Rinpoche: What do you mean, 'demigod'? Like a demon?

Crystal Mirror: No . . .

Rinpoche: You mean, like God?

Crystal Mirror: Yes.

Rinpoche: Well, some people may have that kind of vision, internal dream. They may think many things, but that's their own fantasy.

Crystal Mirror: At what point in a person's spiritual progress does he really need a guru, and why?

Rinpoche: Some people who have attained some realization, perhaps through art or music, or possibly drugs, if they have become totally liberated, they may not necessarily need a guru. But those people are very rare. Most people, I think, can benefit very much from instruction. Traditionally within Buddhism a guru is usually necessary.

But a qualified guru is difficult to find. In Tibet they say, "Do-med yul-la kyuk-gyu; na-do mu-phen ka med." If dogs are threatening you and there are no rocks, then throw clods of dirt. Even though a properly qualified guru may not exist, we need to pretend. That's the situation.

Crystal Mirror: You are trying to establish a firm base for Vajrayāna Buddhism in this country. How compatible is this form of Buddhism with America's culture and people?

Rinpoche: Buddhism was first introduced into this country from Japan. Maybe ten years ago it was very popular. But many people tell me Americans are now more interested in Vajrayāna.

I think Vajrayāna has much color and exciting teachings; philosophy, rituals, and much creative activity. It seems

Americans like that, especially the young people. So I think it can very possibly work here.

Crystal Mirror: This is a time characterized by many social, economic, and political problems, and it sometimes seems futile to attempt finding any solution. Do you agree with this?

Rinpoche: Yes. I think all these social and political problems are based on human suffering, such as desires and ego struggles, individual emotions, ignorance—principally these. I don't think we can improve that situation politically. But I believe that individually each individual needs to strive to understand and communicate with other people, to share. For instance, here in this house we have fewer expenses than if we lived as individuals separately. More important is communication and understanding each other—not fighting.

Politically, well, I think it is important to keep friendship and to accept one another within groups, like among friends and family, or within groups of people living together. For instance, if someone is very hurt or emotional one day, if the moodiness is very high, then he needs to be given consideration because he is like that, *that* day. You need to accept him that way, to understand . . . .

We cannot make everything perfect politically. One person cannot do this, unless maybe he is a great Bodhisattva. Maybe someone has a good idea, but when he sets out to solve the problems, the solution is not quite right; there is still something missing. Because we are human beings, we cannot give the answer. So basically, as individuals we can live simply, without confusions, with understanding and satisfaction. That is how life should be. That's what I believe.

Crystal Mirror: You have been in a number of countries. Why did you choose to teach in America, and specifically in Berkeley, California?

Rinpoche: I have been in Paris, in England, Scotland, New York, and various states in America. Well, I chose to stay in this country.

Many people don't like America. They say it's like a child, a new country, materialistic, with pollution and big problems, a violent country. They say Americans are only interested in sex and dope. But I feel that Americans—particularly young people—have a true heart. There is sincerity and there is much interest in truth and spiritual life. So I have much hope.

Tibet no longer exists, so the traditions, teachings as passed through many generations, the translations, the work of very, very many years, this is almost lost. It needs to be preserved. I think Tibetan Buddhism is very suited to America, because Americans need Dharma. There is suffering and dissatisfaction here. People are looking for a happier life and asking questions.

Before I first came here no one knew the Vajra Guru mantra, or had heard of Padmasambhava. But since I came to America there are lots, I may say hundreds of people praying the Vajra Guru mantra. Also, they understand what Vajrayāna means, at least on a very basic level. So my most encouraging experience has been in America. Particularly this area. In some ways it has many radicals, and many terrible things happening, but on the other hand there are many smart people, and many open people. Some may ask, "Why do you come to the worst place—California, and particularly Berkeley?" But I think it's important that I am here. The experience—we've been here three years—is all right. I believe everything is fine; I think it's okay.

On Thoughts

If wandering thoughts keep on arising,
Catch hold of your Self-mind with alertness.
Be attached neither to samsara nor nirvana,
But rest yourself at ease in full Equality.
Let what arises rise:
Take care not to follow.

Milarepa

As soon as we start to say something, meditation is destroyed. As soon as we start to conceptualize, at that moment, the meditation experience runs away. And yet, without saying something, without examining, it doesn't seem satisfying. So, to feel that we understand, we use verbal symbols. That is our nature—we use words to express things, to give measurement: It's like this; it's like that. We have ideas: It's not like this; it's not like that.

But finally we become blocked. We can't express real meaning, so we become frustrated. We think that we can't know something unless we can measure it. But really, the only simple way is to go directly into the situation, to see it, be it, and then express it. Then, some sort of understanding or experience may come through this narrow channel.

So how do we break this shell of conception? How can we crack our own thoughts? This shell confines, as gravity pulls down. Thoughts in a way have gravity. They pull with tremendous force, characteristic of our dual mind. On the surface of the ocean there are many heavy waves. But this is a surface phenomenon. If you go down just twenty feet, it's very quiet, very calm, very still. It's the same with our minds. In the outer form of one thought, many forces are active. Go further in and there is stillness—you can find it in the thought. There is no distraction left.

Our mind or thoughts are always running here and there, rapidly changing. We cannot still or relax our mind, and so we cannot focus on it. In meditation we try to find a consciousness different from this usual state of mind.

Basically, there are two ways to approach the mind. One is intellectual: We examine and analyze it. Forget these things. Concepts have limits. We want to try to deal with mind and thought directly. The opposite approach is to try to scare away all thoughts, or maybe tranquilize them so that meditation becomes a big vastness: no thoughts, no concepts, very peaceful, very still.

But there is also a different way. It is possible to make the thought itself meditation. Most of the time, our problems are really thoughts—our emotions and judgments make us disturbed. But the substance of thought itself can become meditation. As thoughts come, limitations, fixations, and judgments are set up. But if our awareness is in the center of thought, the thought itself dissolves. The mind is completely aware, completely balanced.

How do we go into that state? The moment you try to separate yourself from thought, you are dealing with duality, a subject-object relationship. You lose the state of awareness because you reject your experience and become separate from it. You are trying to catch a rainbow: It seems close, and at the same time you can't reach it. Mind is sensitive, like radar, dividing reality into hundredths of seconds. It always needs relationships, objects, this and that. It needs something to touch, and cannot survive alone. But there is a way to go into true stillness, where no one is holding, where no one is preparing meditation, where no one is left out. This state is all inclusive: Nothing is left other than meditation or, you could say, complete awareness, complete dance.

Before Conceptualization

With any kind of thought or form, you have a range of mental activities going on. Before the specific activity of conceptualization, you can be in the thought and you can stay in it . . . within the moment, within that very first state. At the very beginning, almost nothing moves. Stay in the concepts, the thoughts. Just be there. You can do this, and it automatically becomes meditation, automatically becomes balance, automatically becomes awareness. There is no need for any support, or knowledge, or any instructions, or anybody. There is nothing left outside 'you'. You become the center of the thought. But there is not really any center—the center becomes balance. There is no 'being', no 'object-subject relationships': None of these categories exist. Yet at the same time, there is functionality, there is complete openness.

The beauty of your own nature allows you to exercise with these things: within thought, within concepts. First, a thought comes: "Okay, I see it. . . ." Thought may sometimes hypnotize me completely, so that I completely swallow it: I become the thought. But sometimes the thought may not completely block me, and I can see it, but I cannot get free. The thoughts are there, always pulling me back. Sometimes thoughts pull at your legs: You have no way to free yourself, no liberation—it's like being tied up. Or sometimes thoughts build a wall: You can't see anything other than that thought.

Sometimes you yourself become the thought. "I am the thought." It seems we have little control over our thoughts.

The one who is practicing, the meditator, is trying to see: "A thought is coming . . . now it's coming, be careful." You try to push it back; it goes back and forth. Sometimes you win, sometimes you lose. But we don't realize *who it is* that is pushing. That one: that's another kind of thought manifestation. Your own mind is tricking you. Who is pushing? That's another kind of thought. And then it's back and forth again, pulling and pushing. It takes a long time to realize that all of this is a game.

A very wise person, who has great experience, will come to realize that all of it is a game—just tricks. You're playing mind games, many inner dialogues. Later on you realize how you've been wasting time. For many years of meditation you've been doing things perfectly, giving lots of effort—but, you know, it's a waste of time, of no value. You don't realize that it's always the thought's game—that by going along, you are actively tricking yourself.

We go on like this, not realizing what is happening, and gradually we become old. Children are so fascinated by their own games, but then they become older and wiser, and though they still enjoy them, they know they're not truly real. In the same way, as you find maturity in your own practice, you see that all this pushing and pulling, all these games, are the same family. There are no differences.

In time you become less interested in these games. Thoughts come, or they don't come . . . emotions come, or they don't come . . . . You do not become so fixated on them. As you mature, you develop a big mind. You don't care so much. Your mind becomes less narrow. At this point, if you become skillful, you can go *into* the thought—into the front of it, or into the back of it, or into the one making the judgments about it: "This is good; this is not good." Maybe you can embrace that judgmental one who is you trying to discriminate; maybe you can become united with that judging mind.

So we 'crack' each thought, like cracking nuts. If we can do this, any thought becomes meditation. Any mental activity, any situation, can be transcended, and you can reach a state of balance. Negative characteristics are lost, or transcended—they become a form of meditation. At that time, they no longer exist as ordinary or samsaric mind. Ordinary consciousness has been transformed, but how this happens is very subtle, almost paradoxical. Because as soon as you try to do this, to do anything at all, immediately this is a second state—the next thought, or state of mind. Mind changes so quickly. So you need to very carefully develop 'skillful means'.

Trying hard is not effective in meditation. Instead, be confident and don't try to mold your practice into a perfect pattern. We say, "Oh, this is not concentration . . . this is not the right way . . . this must be something else." You don't need to use your energy in this way, conceptually, giving names, always expressing yourself to yourself. Forget about concepts. Get away from trying to identify—"Is this wisdom? or awareness? or meditation? or God-consciousness? Is it this? Is it that?" Don't try to make anything into anything.

You don't need to worry about whether this experience you are having is good or bad or right or wrong. All these responses are judgments. Don't worry and don't give power to judgments. Just forget it, absolutely forget it. Just be *in* there, following your own kind of openness—any thought, any time. There is no special time. Any time there is a thought or activity, just be. Don't try to escape; don't try to ignore; don't try to do anything. Do nothing. Does that mean escaping? No—no one is escaping. No one is trying to do anything. You can become centerlessness, with no subject, no object, nothing in between. The nature of reality cannot be reached by trying hard.

The Subtle Nature of Mind

At first, as you gain experience, you feel, "Ah, I can see . . . . There is a place I have reached . . . . Now I can see very subtle distinctions." But once you really find that place, it is infinite—bigger than this universe. This world, this universe as we conceive it, is all included within that state of consciousness, that underlying nature. And that nature is completely centerless. In one way, everything is included, and in another way, nothing really is in it.

This is the subtle nature of mind. In one sense it is infinite, and in another sense it is very limited. In this world, whatever exists has limits—form has limits, knowledge has limits, ordinary consciousness has limits. But from another view, there are no limits—not even the distinction between limits and limitlessness exists.

Often we may think, "Okay now, I would like to express something verbally. Conceptually, I'd like to make a model of this, to bring something out or to give information." This is part of the distraction of the individual ego. "I have discovered new things. I want to report it to myself. I'm excited." This is samsaric mind, getting excited over concepts. The mind makes patterns: "This is my idea, my life, my world, my country, my culture." So many things. "*I've* named it, *I've* labeled it, *I've* made up these shapes, *I* did it."

Actually these are just mental discriminations, projections. What underlies all of this? We say that all existence is made up of atoms, or of energy, or some indefinable combination of these concepts. Well, what is our consciousness made of? Actually, it is all the same reality, the same energy. Our consciousness or mind is made up of the infinite. In meditation, it becomes self-manifested.

Perhaps you have problems accepting this. You think God is very high, Buddha is very high, enlightenment is very far from you. No one can reach nirvana, and besides, you are dominated by a lower person, a sinful, negative, impure person. But these blockages all just come from discrimination. Thoughts come and interrupt: "That is not possible. . . . This doctrine says. . . . Intellectually, it could not be." You make it more difficult for yourself with so many discriminations and negative judgments. If you don't accept it, you cannot taste it, cannot see it. When you cannot taste it, you lose confidence. Then you are on the outside of nirvana, the outside of the nature of Buddha. On the other side, you may think, "If nirvana is that simple, than I am already in nirvana." But as soon as I *think* I am in nirvana, then I am not in nirvana. Even if I try to pretend, and don't say anything, that doesn't help either.

We do not really know where we are or who we are. We have concepts of nirvana, enlightenment, God-consciousness, or infinity, but our ideas are very restricted. Intellectually we have given everything a shape. We have civilized everything intellectually—and so we can find nothing. We almost cannot think about, say, or do anything.

Samsara and Nirvana

In Buddhism, there is only a very subtle distinction between samsara and nirvana. There aren't really any differences between the world and heaven. It's only a matter of realizing or not realizing it. And whether we realize it or not, or reach that state or not, depends on very little, because there's really no difference between the two. It's even difficult to know which side of the coin is realization and which is not realization—they're both the same coin. If one side of the coin is not there, the other side can't be there. If the front side of my hand doesn't exist, the back side cannot exist. Similarly, if this consciousness or this mind or this thought does not exist, then my meditation cannot survive, and enlightenment is not possible.

That meditation, that nirvana, is so close—there is no time and distance. We have words naming this, but they're only words. When there is no time or distance, we can say 'nowness', this very moment, the presence of your mind, the presence of your thought. An ancient Buddhist illustration shows a circle: One part is nirvana, one part is samsara. The moment you can go *into* that circle, you are enlightened. There are many diagrams and symbolic drawings to show the practitioner how close 'nowness' is—that there is really no distance to it.

We are always within it—just as we are now. We are not separated from that reality. We're not separated from meditation. Our mind is not separate from Buddha nature. But due to a lack of understanding, due to not-knowing, our thought-forms as they usually operate are clouded or deluded. We also have all kinds of conflicting emotions and negativity, which are characteristic of samsara. Because of these obscurations we see enlightenment as small, something at a distance. It doesn't even seem substantial—it's like a soap bubble. But we have this idea because we are not *in* it. If we become the inside of the bubble, we find infinity there. But until then we feel this way or that way, always judging, because the nature of the mind as we know it is dual.

There is a children's story about a sea tortoise and a frog. The tortoise comes from a distance to see the frog, who lives in a very, very small lake. And they talk to each other.

"Where do you come from?"

"I come from the ocean."

"What is that?"

"It's like . . . well . . . It's like the *ocean*."

"Can you explain to me what the ocean is? Here, where I live," says the frog, "This is so big. Can you explain how big the ocean is? Is it half this size? Is it full size?"

And the tortoise says, "More than that. The ocean is much bigger than where you live."

But the frog has only a limited experience—he cannot believe that there is anywhere bigger than his lake. There is no way to describe to him how big the ocean is. So the tortoise brings the frog to the ocean to show him how big it is. And the frog is so astounded by the *vastness* . . . he almost faints.

We say we live in samsara, or we live in the Kāli Yuga, a time of great depression, negativity, and all kinds of problems. But in the darkest time, the light is more bright than at any other time. Even during the worst possible depression, or when the worst things happen, the light shines. It shines within a thought. You can find it—your true guide is there. Your true teacher, the teaching, is your own realization, and that's your real father, your guide, your teaching, your knowledge, your wisdom. You don't need to worry about your body or your thoughts. Everything is perfect.

This is not just an idea or fantasy. Everything *is* perfect. Even though someone breaks a leg or has problems, even though it's difficult, and wires get crossed, and there's an energy crisis, and an economic problem, and people can't get jobs, and everybody has many complaints . . . still, the essence of your own consciousness can become peace. Your head can be clear, and then the world may not disturb you.

Perhaps it is true that as long as you exist in a samsaric condition, you have to face and deal with problems, have to work them out. But looking at the mind, who is working? Who is working in this world? Who created it? The answer is, our thoughts. A child may ask, "Who created this whole world?" and we may answer God, or so-and-so, or karma, but actually, our thoughts created it.

Whatever we have going on in our consciousness is good 'stuff'. It's very useful; we can work with it. The Dharma speaks of a path. What is a path? What is practice? Path, stages—Why do we need these things? Why do we need to practice? Because we have thoughts. Practice is *thought*; practice is experience. As long as there is thought, we need to practice. When there are no longer thought-forms, when this is transcended, there is no path, no road to follow, not even any goal or results. The path is only thought. When there are no thought-forms, there is nothing left. What is has become its own reality, its 'thatness.' It has become reality itself.

In a way, the path is so simple: As long as you have thought, as long as you have concepts, that's your path. There seem to be many differences, and even conflicting approaches, in Buddhist practices and doctrines. But as long as you have thought, that's your path; that's your practice. Thought itself is practice.

Many people talk of happiness, or enjoyment, or satisfaction, but it's only an idea. When one day you really have it, then you know. You're convinced. You don't even need to express how it is—the question doesn't arise. You don't care whether somebody approves or disapproves. You don't care too much in that way, you're not anxious, because you *know*, and this knowing is the highest there is.

You Are the One

If you go into your thought, what the thought creates is really 'me'. I am the subject who creates 'I am', the judge who makes heaven and hell, ascending and descending. When you realize this you become a truly powerful person. You can go wherever you want—the horrible places, the beautiful places, the heavenly places—and everywhere you are blissful, because every aspect is so beautiful. It's all in the receiver or perceiver, the one who is relating to it, the one who is 'I am'.

There is no one more important than yourself. This may sound very egotistical, but that is how it is. You can completely dominate yourself, make yourself a complete prisoner—or you can completely liberate yourself.

We say that something makes me happy: a beautiful woman, a beautiful man, a beautiful home, lots of money, a rich country. But actually our thoughts create our world. If you carefully examine, nothing else really makes you happy, none of these other conditions really affect you. You are the one who decides how you want to react to any situation or relationship. That's the way it works.

In this life, we can do just so much. We cannot physically change everything in the world, but our own energy, our being: This we can change. We have nothing more important than our 'beingness'—our own selves. As human beings, we can develop this through our own growth. Meditation is this live growth, this potential.

You need to encourage yourself, because you have much great potential. We love to travel to Europe, Asia, and different countries—one day it may be that we will want to travel to the moon or Mars, or to different planets. But if you travel in wider consciousness, travel in meditation, there are many different realms. I am not exaggerating: It's faster than flying in a plane. In a moment, a second, you can go into consciousness and discover a different realm. Or at least you can find a different experience.

Always Within

Sometimes we may be concerned with death, or with losing ourselves, or loneliness, or leaving this world. But some things are more basic than this. We may be able to go here and there in space, but all the scientists in the world working together cannot go *beyond* space. No matter what, we are always 'within'. We always belong to the Buddha-field, or God-consciousness, or Infinite Mind. In this sense we are always united. There are many names for this being within a whole: God, Jesus Christ, Buddha, Enlightenment.

All these names have the same root, and they are all available right now. We tend to look at history and interpret something as finished in this world: It is already done, and today is something else. Today we are here. But if I speak truly, *they—these ones we name—are here too.* If they are truly enlightened, they are within everything—they have not gone anywhere. For example, Jesus Christ nailed to the cross is very symbolic: He is not separate. Samsara and nirvana, illusion and reality, are integrated, inseparable. And we too are already within that nature.

We are sometimes so lonely and sad . . . but we are not alone. Within our own awareness, there are many good friends. Even if we want to, we cannot separate ourselves from them. Still, we may have many fears. But to start, we can remind ourselves that what we fear will change. These things are not permanent.

This is an example of how we can make friends with our own deeper realization, the best friend we can have. Whenever we have problems, we can ask for advice, and we will get positive, helpful answers. In the moment of suffering, we can ask our own realization and find encouragement, inspiration, and the path to enlightenment. We are often lonely and sometimes desperate. At these times, we must really encourage ourselves: Our real family, our true home, is within. We can change difficult feelings into positive feelings of love.

How much we love entertainments and nice things. But once mind is transformed, any aspect of experience—sound, form, friends . . . every object in the world—becomes very beautiful. Everything shines. Everything becomes beauty, or art, or music. For instance, sometime you may be very surprised at *sound*, at how it is. Even when you listen to your own voice, there is something you can learn from it. Someone is internally communicating with you, and this experience can give you knowledge. Even just looking at the leaves of a small plant can make something very clear to you. Every single aspect of existence becomes a kind of beauty and a knowing. There is something you can learn from each experience. As your consciousness becomes transformed, natural insight develops.

Since we are always within that true nature, we can always rely on it completely. No matter what struggles or problems we have, we are still within the positive realm. When we understand that level of consciousness, we see we are in the very safest place. You may say we are in samsara, but samsara is within reality. The enlightened seed is there, and we are in that seed.

If we look to our own true nature we can always see the positive side. We don't need to worry too much, or be too concerned. We have to face many difficulties, but all of them are a manifestation of our thoughts and concepts. At any time we can go into our thoughts, and the problems will dissolve, like a bubble.

Bringing the Teachings Alive

The teachings and our selves are not separate. Still, we have made mistakes, interpreted the doctrines or teachings wrongly. We have categorized things so very strictly that we have drifted far from the Buddha's teachings. Today, because of these many unclear interpretations, we do not really understand the teachings. We say, "Not this, not that." We divide everything. We may say, "There is one beautiful divine nature." But even that is cut up conceptually, negated logically, until there is almost nothing left. Then that divine nature is far away. Negation is just our own concepts. Work with negative concepts for a long, long time, and finally you get nothing.

We have many ideas about the teachings, doctrines, and interpretations. But first they are sound. Our own voice is a teaching: The sound we make is the doctrine, our own interpretation is the teaching. The teaching is introduced in order to realize something, but the teaching and the realization are not separate. You may have many problems, but if you can bring the teachings alive in this way, awareness becomes fresh, alive within your own thought. This quality of aliveness is like light, so therefore we call it enlightened. It is just wisdom—no feelings of separation, just completely free, completely positive, with no problems and no negation that divides and destroys. The characteristics of samsaric mind are no longer present. The mind becomes completely balanced. That is what meditation finally means, and this is what we need to practice.

Any moment, wherever you are, driving a car, sitting around, working, talking, any activities at all—even if you are very disturbed emotionally, very passionate, very depressed, even if your mind has become very strong, raging, overcome with the worst possible things and you cannot control yourself—if you really go into it, there's nothing there. Whatever comes up becomes your meditation. The more heated up you are, the more energy there is. Even if the tension builds, if you go into your thought and your awareness becomes alive, that moment can be more powerful than working for a long time on meditation practice. At those times, a short moment can bring great results.

There is nothing to throw away—even the most negative emotions are useful. The more you go into the disturbance—

when you really get in there—the emotional characteristics no longer exist. Then this becomes proper meditation. Your experience becomes part of your realization.

If you look in a subject-object way, then you have problems. But if you really get into it, then there is nothing left—no anger, no greed, no lust. These are words which are terrible, negative, bitter—you don't even mention them. But even with these lower emotions, it's possible you can heat them up and stay in them. Maybe you can't find anything there at all.

When you practice in this way, don't lose the center. Go into the thought. When you're in that state, everything heated up, stay in the meditation. Soon the meditation becomes very powerful. I think that is what is sometimes called a peak experience—not the absolute experience, but a really good experience.

Whenever you have distraction, go into it. Don't separate yourself from it. Don't separate yourself from your ego and that emotion. This way you become one, go *into* one. Bring up as much fire, energy, as you can, and stay in it. Don't go away from it, and don't separate yourself from it. You and your experience become united. Stay in it, be in it, be *still* in it. Don't judge it; just express it, but stay still within it. It may be very, very useful.

We have a hard time facing things. We are always trying to escape, always running away from things. And we are tight. . . . we hang on. We understand, in a way, what reality is, but on the other hand, we are living today in samsara, and we have to be concerned with various things: with work, with society, with parents, with our reputation, our own name, with morality, and so on. We are tied up in every way, like prisoners. Samsara is our prison, so there can be no freedom. Even in our own concepts, we don't think freely, because the mind is too tight, too caught in judging and wanting. If we think one way, we feel guilty: "Oh, I shouldn't think about that." If we think another way, we just generate more thoughts, more wanting.

These things happen in the human condition. But still you can exercise, you can work with thoughts. Do the exercise—do it secretly, in a way—and get into the experience. You have to learn to do this, because you cannot hide for a whole lifetime. You have to face it—whatever 'it' is—sometime. Facing it may be better than hiding, ignoring, or trying to escape.

All these things, all these difficulties—start from thought. Thought is so simple. So work with it. Past thought, present thought, future thought—anytime at all—go into the thought. This becomes your meditation.

When we say, "You cannot contemplate, you cannot concentrate," we are making enemies of our thoughts. This is what we want to break down. Let go of the judgments that thoughts make—you don't need to cross that bridge. We can become completely relaxed. Mind becomes still and free, and that is our meditation.

Transmuting Energies through Breath

There is tranquility and insight
In relying on the real foundation of life
Because of fusing mind with mind
And discriminating the whole of reality.
                    Mahāyāna-sūtrālaṁkāra

We can transmute negative feelings into positive, balanced feelings. This does not mean just trying to be happy, because happiness is not necessarily balanced. The feeling of balance is something quite different.

Negativity is often based on frustration, but frustration itself can be transmuted. The key is whether mind and breath are functioning properly. When breath is not balanced, many thoughts and concepts arise, and this leads directly to frustration and negativity. So it is very important to become conscious of the breath.

When the breath is balanced, it is like an expansive lake with very still water. Left alone, the lake reflects the things around it very beautifully. But if we disturb the lake by throwing a rock into it, a clear and beautiful image can no longer form. Watching our breath, we can see whether it is still and balanced. If it is out of balance, then by watching with care, we can discover what disturbs us.

There are actually two types of breath. The first is the outer breath, which is our normal breathing pattern. When a person really begins to enter into meditation, this outer breath almost disappears. At this time there is no feeling of tension, as if the breath had somehow been taken away. It is felt more as a loss of roughness in the outer breath. An inner breath emerges, soft and calm—a very relaxed form of breathing that we do not need to think about. It is very enjoyable, comfortable, and full of feeling—soothing, with a quality of quietness.

There is very important energy in this inner breath, and to become balanced we must learn how to develop it. But the inner breath is so easy to lose. If you want to prevent this, resolve not to waste the breath. Breathe quietly and use your breath as little as possible. Then you can learn to see in what ways you are spending this precious resource.

Mostly we spend our breath verbalizing. As we talk, each word we use goes to our thoughts. Used in this way, the breath is like a horse: It tires as it runs. If we carefully watch when we speak, we can see how our energy level is drained. So this is a first guide: Use as little energy as possible in verbalizing.

Often it is necessary to communicate with others, and there is no real harm in this. But if we simply use our breath in verbal speculation, for no real purpose, our energy will collapse into depression. Yesterday something particular happened, today we find we need to repeat it verbally, and tomorrow we will need to explain things that happened today. This kind of speculation can circulate endlessly. It can continue our whole lives, leading nowhere.

Verbal speculation not only wastes energy—it causes us much unhappiness. In listening to ourselves or others, we agree or disagree. Soon opinions form. We are caught up in arguments, and we have positions to defend. The natural outcome is conflict and negativity. Instead of responding to our situation in an open and balanced way, we move toward negativity.

There is another kind of speculation that is also linked to the breath, even though it is not verbal. This is image-like speculation. A picture forms in our minds, and then another. Perhaps we comment on the images or react to them, moving once more toward verbal speculation. But as long as the images draw us in, we live in an artificial world. We are living in our minds, using the energy of the head, cut off from the world in which our lives are unfolding.

The body has within it various chakras, centers for emotions, feelings, and energy. If we channel energy properly through all these centers, certain positive reactions are automatically produced. To do this, we need to transmute these energies in a positive way through learning not to waste the breath, but to make use of it effectively.

The less we waste the breath, the more still it becomes, and the more we grow calm. It is this calm, inner breath that we can transmute into something blissful. As we relax into it, we discover a kind of pure energy that has great value or potential. To make this discovery can lead us to a new source of meaning and can produce tremendous positive feelings.

When the soft inner breath is linked to concentration, it can flow to all parts of the body, circulating through the cakras and removing all kinds of blockages. This can happen in less than one second: The inner breath moves that fast.

Developing the subtle, inner breath can make us tranquil. It can completely relieve us of all our tensions or blockages, all the negative emotions that make us so rigid. We have learned to think that we have only one way of being, that fundamentally there are no solutions to our problems. Thinking this way, we don't want to move, we don't want to open, we don't want to accept. We do not even want to think in any other way. We become absolutely rigid. In the end we may despair, even to the point of considering suicide, because there is just no way out.

Conventionally, we try to deal with this kind of situation through new thoughts, new insights, perhaps new experiences. But this is to stay on the same level. There may be a much simpler way, one that we begin to touch as soon as we learn to control our breath.

If we seriously want to explore this possibility, we must learn to work with the breath from the beginning. Before anything happens, before we react, we just keep the breath very calm, very soft . . . little movement, not too much action. This is not too difficult, because this kind of breathing gives a very soothing and pleasant feeling, producing warmth in various degrees. As we continue to concentrate on this breathing, our bodies can become completely relaxed. Then experience becomes very different from what we had thought it was.

This simple practice offers a unique way to transmute blockages into very blissful, very sensitive feelings. The feeling and the breath become like partners in a marriage. Positive feelings, blissful feelings, enjoyable, inexpressible feelings . . . all are contained in the soft, inner breath. Just focus on this breath. As you touch it, so that experience shifts, bring the feelings and breath into union. In time, all the rest will come.

Waking Up to Infinite Possibilities

Every single thought, every moment of experience, has a silent nature within it that we can contact directly. If we understand this silent, meditative quality, there is no need to fight or subdue anything or anyone.

The quickest way to enlightenment is through meditation. Meditation allows us to challenge our problems directly, so that we can ease any tension or friction between our experience, our intellectual knowledge, and the knowledge of our hearts. Once we have cleaned our karma in this way, we can touch our pure nature directly. We can discover the perfect meditative quality that is always there, in every moment of our lives.

This is why enlightenment can happen in any moment. The degree of our experience, our age, our sex or other personal characteristics have no bearing at all. The usual procedure is to seek enlightenment by learning and studying for a long time, but it can also happen that you go to bed one night and wake up the next morning enlightened. This may be how it goes.

Until we begin with meditation, the knowledge we learn is likely to consist mainly of information rather than direct experience. True, we have experience, but this experience simply forms the background for affirming or rejecting already established concepts and images.

Meditation can get us beyond conceptual knowledge to the genuine nature of mind. No one, not even the Buddha, can give us this direct experience, but meditation can do it. The Buddha can show us what to do, but we have to take responsibility to do it for ourselves. This is why we say that money and property and power can end, but meditation is an infinite treasure. It is there and it is reliable; we can take refuge in it at any time.

Some types of meditation instruction say, "Sit till your legs grow numb," but this technique is similar to having a stubborn nature—forceful, rigid, narrow. It reflects an approach to life, a judgment that life is a fight. It is true that from the time we were born, fighting has been a large part of our lives. Often we feel that there is something wrong that we must resist, some stand we have to take. But as we come to understand meditation, we realize that there is nothing to fight. Once we have realization, we understand that every single thought, every moment of experience, has a silent nature within it that we can contact directly. If we understand this silent, meditative quality, there is no need to fight or subdue anything or anyone. There is nothing to do but to *be*, and to be completely open.

There are several ways to develop meditation. The first is the gradual way: We can sit for ten minutes or so without thoughts or concepts; later, we can extend this time further. But a quicker way is to see the problem or pain right at the beginning, and right then to open to it, so that it instantly *becomes* meditation. Whereas the gradual way is a cleaning up, so that there are no more problems, the second way—the more 'esoteric' way—is not a cleaning or cleansing at all. It is working with what is there directly, whether it is emotions, negativities, ego, or desire. The enemy and the antidote work together.

There is also a third kind of meditation, based on an understanding even broader than this. This way reaches beyond duality, even beyond working with things 'together', because that approach is still oriented toward subject and object. This level transcends any categorizing of experience. We see that there is no substance to either positive or negative, happiness or unhappiness. The truth of every experience shines forth.

These different teachings are appropriate for different levels of consciousness. Each teaching has a positive effect, but the higher teachings have greater results. But although the higher teachings may sound good to us, they cannot help us if we are not ready for them. And if we force ourselves, trying to practice in accord with a way for which we are not naturally ready, that forcing can create yet another agitation. The mind has a very strong energy, and if we let that energy be guided by the feeling that our meditation has to be perfect, it may prove dangerous. Because we will never be satisfied, we may wind up with even more problems than when we started.

It is most helpful to apply teachings on meditation, at whatever level, without demands or expectations. When we don't take positions the energy flows. Once we cease seeking, we can rest directly in our experience. Then growth will come of its own accord, and with it, complete understanding will unfold.

When meditative awareness is integrated with our bodies, minds, and senses, meditation can be used to cope with our daily problems. And those problems in turn can become part of our meditation. How quickly this happens depends on our karmic circumstances and obligations and on our psychological patterns. As positive attitudes are created and our negative emotions lose their hold on us, growth can occur day by day.

We can further this development by reminding ourselves to look at what is going on. Whatever your activity, just ask, "Hey, what are you doing?" The moment you look, the meditative quality is there. In the beginning, try to look for a few minutes and to repeat this several times a day. Gradually do it more often and for longer periods, until your meditative awareness becomes so strong that you can carry it even into your dreams.

Eventually there is no space other than meditation. If an emotion comes and takes over your consciousness, it lasts only for a short time; you can wake up immediately. You become like a dancer who has practiced for fifteen years: She may fall down, but she can quickly get on her feet again. In the same way, the experienced meditator can support himself or herself and balance any experience easily. Over time, the reminding no longer comes as a shock; it happens naturally, and no extra effort is needed. What begins as a technique becomes a natural way of being. There is no separation between you and the meditation.

The more meditative awareness arises, the more sensitive and awakened we become. The awakened state increases the light available, until we can see and know everything: There are no dark corners. Meditative awareness is perfect wisdom and will awaken any situation.

From this broader perspective, our problems seem very small indeed. In fact, we realize that being overly concerned with our problems is just a way of cheating ourselves by making ourselves weak. Problems stem from seeing things only our own way, from taking a narrow perspective. But until our perspective opens, we cannot truly awaken our awareness.

Through meditation, we can polish the mind and give it a radiant, gem-like quality. We can tap a tremendous potential that will let us contribute to the harmony of the world. It is really quite simple: Through taking the medicine of meditation we can take care of ourselves, and if we can take care of ourselves, we gain positive experience and knowledge that we can share with others. Opening our hearts, at first to a few friends and then perhaps more broadly, we can make the privilege of being born in this world worthwhile.

For these benefits to develop, we must first develop confidence. Our habit patterns are tremendously powerful and may be difficult to give up. But with the awareness that comes through meditation, we gain access to a new source of power, based on knowledge. Communication between ourselves and the rest of the world improves, and from this arises a deep sense of understanding that ripens into trust. Ultimately, this trust will lead to an experience of reality as it is—the one truth of what we might call absolute nature. Although we have been separate for a long time, we can go back to the original, uncreated reality, for it is also a part of ourselves. Perhaps we call it 'God' or 'peak experience' or 'enlightened mind': Such terms will in any case only impose limitations. Whatever it is, we can contact it directly through meditation.

Meditation is confronting what comes, not following information, instructions, or ideals. Assumptions or descriptions about what meditation or enlightenment is are not real. True knowledge comes through experience. Once we clean up our thoughts, we can experience what is there and know who we are. With that knowledge, we can direct ourselves and heal our deceptions.

As an effective path toward realization, meditation is not any kind of fixation. It is simply a way of unlocking or opening all of our experience. But it may be hard to stay with this simplicity. Whenever we begin something, we tend to project specific goals, and this is true when we begin to meditate. Psychologically, anxiety has already started on a subtle level, and we can easily trap ourselves in the idea that we can or should be getting something. We hope to attain our goal and fear that we will not; holding on to our hopes and fears, we cannot relax and appreciate our experience, and the road to growth is blocked.

If we let go of our goal orientation, all this shifts. We can understand that the world, just as it is, is interesting and valuable—rich with all kinds of experiences that we can enjoy and benefit from. We do not have to accept any one experience as being more right than any other. Sometimes we have peak experiences; at other times we feel depressed or completely lost—it moves in cycles, and we can move with it. Thus, experience itself will reveal to us the times we need to meditate. There will be moments in each day when suddenly we have a happy, light mind, and other moments when we are confused and dull. These are the times to test our concentration and relaxation, to ask what we are doing. It is more important to cultivate meditative awareness at these times than to practice formal meditation at specific times of the morning and evening.

The point is to appreciate each moment as fully as possible—whatever comes. This does not mean that we forget the future, but it does mean that the goal, the fruit, is already here. We could spend our whole lives slowly starving to death, selling the present for the future and getting nothing nourishing in return. But we can also do it differently. Through a refined searching and inquiry, through watching our own minds, we can learn great lessons. The silent space between thoughts is always available. The unborn is always there, and 'there' is not a place. Here, as always, language is a gesture or symbol. If we can use the symbols to cross over, there are very important meanings behind them, on the other side.

This lifetime presents us with a valuable opportunity to embody a healthy way of being and to awaken the mind. The Dharma shows us how to do this. In this sense Buddhism is not necessarily religious; instead it is a way of life. Practicing the Dharma, our life becomes a work of art.

The most precious resource we have is our energy, both mental and physical. Right now we can learn to use this energy economically and productively. Ten or fifteen years from now it may be more difficult: Other circumstances may prevail, and our minds might change. That is why today is so important. This may be the most precious opportunity we ever have to wake up to our full potential. We can change our lives. Now is the time.

The Nature of Laziness

With meditative experience, we can see that both laziness and vigor are feelings created by the mind.

The mind of laziness is a dangerous mind, for if you have a mind affected by laziness, you cannot achieve your goal. Laziness has many manifestations. For example, you might want to do something, but then you think, "Now is not the right time. Wait, I will do it later on." Then the time is gone.

Laziness mind creates certain feelings and rationalizations. We say, "Don't worry, I'll help you another time," or "Today we didn't accomplish anything, but tomorrow we will, or some other time." These thoughts produce a kind of pseudo-confidence, because we actually believe that is how it is and will be. This is the nature of laziness.

In Tibetan, laziness is called le-lo. Le-lo can trick and change your mind in many ways. It can nullify your efforts toward any goal. A mind affected by laziness can create and cling to its own self-fixed ideas until you become rooted in laziness.

Suppose someone studying the Dharma says, "I won't do prostrations or meditation or any other discipline. What's the difference; we're all already enlightened, and it's much nicer and easier not to do anything. I'm happy just enjoying my body and mind. Everything is peaceful, but doing practice is harsh and difficult."

These ideas result from laziness. What creates them? The mind affected by laziness fabricates a certain confidence that its view is correct. It gives itself its own ideas and then holds onto them as the truth.

The laziness mind always disturbs and obstructs you. Whatever you try seems hard for you, physically and mentally. Concentration, visualization, chanting, meditation—they all fall prey to this influence. To justify your failure to act, you rationalize, make excuses, postpone still more—on and on. This is le-lo, laziness.

The antidote for le-lo is brtson-'grus. brTson-'grus means perseverance, vigor, determination to keep on until you succeed, without interruption, whatever happens. Such vigor is the most important of all the six perfections, for without it, not even wisdom can succeed. But if you have vigor, not even the defeating frustrations of emotions, doubts, or anxieties can deter you.

The great man's nature proceeds from vigor and strength. He can succeed in whatever he tries to attain. Even if he does not decide quickly to act, once he does, he can do anything, for good or for ill. Someone with this quality is admirable. But more, this kind of perseverance, important in anyone's life, is essential in Dharma studies.

Even if you do not naturally have vigor, you can make yourself be that way. To do so, you should reflect and realize that if you are lazy, you cannot succeed in anything, not in the worldly or material life, and certainly not in the Dharma. Your life will become useless, and in the end miserable.

We are very fortunate to be born without mental or physical difficulties, and since we have this opportunity, we should strive to do useful things. This means above all else striving for spiritual development, first in ourselves and then in others. But if we are lazy, we will simply not get anywhere.

In the past we have spent so much time simply sleeping or furthering our own enjoyment, yet we remain restless and dissatisfied. This is a very great problem for everyone. When we fail to achieve real satisfaction, we become unhappy. The direct cause of this suffering is laziness.

We are always very strongly attached to our feelings. We may not have very strong desires for big things like fortune, name, or success in society. But still we like a kind of peacefulness, an enjoyment that has to do with being attached to ourselves. This desire to remain attached to our feelings is the real laziness nature. It is not 'kindness mind', even though we may feel we are being kind to ourselves. It is not 'wisdom mind' or 'learning mind' or 'achievement mind'. It is just laziness. This inner feeling of laziness is our enemy, and we should combat it with unrelenting vigor.

We like laziness because it is our habit, but we can also learn to act otherwise. To see this, we need to study the mind in meditation. Someone with meditative experience can see that both laziness and vigor are themselves feelings created by the mind; both are the mind's view. There is no difference at all in their nature.

But at the same time, there is a big difference in the results they produce. Vigor can lead to success in meditation and in whatever we undertake. Laziness leads to failure. That is the difference. Seeing that, can we choose how we wish to act?

The Prize of
True Understanding

However much emphasis and delight we attach to our bodily sensations or mental delights, our pleasures and satisfactions cannot be preserved and stored.

If we were ever truly mindful of how fleeting life is; if we fully experienced the relevance of this general proposition in our own lives, then lethargy would have no hold on us. We would interpret far fewer states of affairs as problems, and the few we did acknowledge would not seem so very discouraging after all.

Seeing death fast approaching, we understand that nothing we are asked to do in life is really too difficult for us. All that we are called upon to do and to face, the pain and the pleasure, take on a new significance. Their value diminishes. Meditation and other spiritual practices are no great hardship; our problems dissolve like the breath when it leaves the body, dispersing naturally in the ten directions.

Suppose our practice is to do one hundred prostrations a day. In the face of the many real hardships and constant suffering in the world, or in the face of our own death, this is not very much to do. And yet we may find it very burdensome; we may use up our energy giving rationalizations for why we cannot do this practice daily. And so it goes with our study and our meditation, with our resolve to be of benefit to others. It is as though with each day the number and importance of our other duties and actions increases. As a result we eventually forsake all Dharma activity.

Why is it that we come to value the Dharma less highly than our responsibilities or our pursuit of pleasure? It seems that we tacitly accept samsara and the limits it imposes on what we can hope to achieve. We tend to think the samsaric condition is 'just human nature'. We think this way because we love ourselves very much, and we are always making room to protect our ego. Accepting our limitations, being 'realistic', gives us a way to justify our action or inaction, our laziness.

We may often observe attachments to the ego at work in someone else, for this is easy to see. But the real egoism is our own, and it is this that should be our only concern. We must realize by looking inside ourselves that the ego is constantly manipulating us and leading us about. In attaching to our ego we give it power, power to keep us in ignorance of our true nature. The more ego attachments that we have, the more we feel a need to make ourselves happy, and the more we assure that happiness remains beyond our reach.

We need to study the ego's workings within us, resisting its attempts to draw our attention outside. Seeking something religious or mystical in externals, rather than within ourselves, is only a distraction. To look inward, with correct understanding—this is the Dharma way. Inside, all the knowledge we need is awaiting discovery.

When our behavior is frivolous, this points to a certain naive confidence that the life and power we now enjoy will never wane. But life is short. What is there about our present understanding of it that justifies this sense of security? What have we possessed or experienced that will always afford us delight or refuge from sorrow? The material world offers us no such thing.

Few people realize the power that desire and pleasure have to enslave them, for they believe both to be good. But what at first seems pleasant quickly leads to misery. Like a sweet-tasting poison, its danger lies in its attractiveness.

If you are awake, you see that most of what we take to be pleasure is really not worth pursuing. To pursue is to be like the moth, drawn by the flame toward its death. We do this out of ignorance. Living in the Kāmadhātu—the desire realm—we do not despise this grasping. No, we love it in all its forms. Money, sex, position . . . . There is no end to the objects of our grasping. But what do we ultimately gain from this frenzied activity? Nothing. It has no meaning.

Can you measure your pleasure? Can it be held, touched, or seen? Does it persist through time? Pleasure, it seems, is not so substantial after all. However much emphasis and delight we attach to our bodily sensations or mental delights, our pleasures and satisfactions cannot be preserved and stored, except as fading memories. One pleasure having lapsed, we seek in our attachment to it to renew it or replace it with another. But the result is just to bind us tightly to anxious craving. We will never be fully satisfied in our searching but will only suffer continual disappointment.

If someone were to understand fully this aspect of samsara, he would wake up to what life means and to what must be done. All this would become very clear. Until now we have been asleep, but we do not have much time left. We must awaken now.

Our initial efforts to wake up may not seem to produce many results. We must pass through at least ten stages of development before we can achieve Enlightenment, so in our initial efforts we may experience great difficulty and discouragement. It is possible to understand only one level at a time. And even if we could take hold of only the first step on this path, we would be most fortunate.

But even though the prize of true understanding may be hard to win, in time it can be done. Then we may see life very differently. Great effort is required, but with the achievement comes the capacity for much self-development and progress.

Situational Patterning: Pratītyasamutpāda

Steven D. Goodman

Becoming's Wheel reveals no known beginning,
No maker, no experiencer there.
Void with a twelvefold voidness,
Nowhere does it ever halt,
Forever does it spin.

Bhadantācāriya Buddhaghosa

Responsiveness, a dynamic and variable function, is an essential characteristic of being human. To be human is always to be in a situation. The experience of one situation after another is one's lived world. We do not use 'world' here in the conventional sense of 'that out there over against which I stand' (an abstracting dualism invoking the ghost dance of the Cartesian *res cogitans* and *res extensa*) but rather in the sense of one's realm of lived meaning.

Every situation, then, is in one way nothing but one's experienced narrowness or limit of meanings. This narrowness, which often entails confusion and bewilderment, is for most people the predominant modality of responsiveness. Stated differently, one might say that much of man's experience is marked by a general and seemingly pervasive unsatisfactoriness. This observation constituted the Lord Buddha's First Truth (duḥkha, sdug-bsngal).

Unlike those who hold that miseries are but random happenings in an indifferent universe ("The silence of infinite space frightens me" —Pascal), Lord Buddha observed that there is a regular patterning to this misery (only loosely to be construed as a cause or origin). This observation constituted the Second Truth (samudaya, kun-'byung). Insight into the nature of this pattern of unsatisfactoriness is a central concern in the teaching of the Buddha. Buddhists believe, along with certain enlightened trends of pragmatism, that a person *can* do something about the quality of his life. This 'doing', however, is not so much just another action among many, but rather the development of a penetrating insight which is appropriate to the situation at hand.

This insight (prajñā, shes-rab) has a dynamic and incisive quality whose tone is always appreciative. It has nothing to do with the development of a cold, searing *logos* carving out larger and larger chunks of a passive world, which as a prominent feature of post-industrial society caused Nietzsche to comment, "In every desire to know there is a drop of cruelty." The development of prajñā is applied directly to one's experience. It may be focused as an analysis of perceptual and cognitive situations, an analysis which always has a preeminently soteriological function. It is *only* developed for the purpose of cutting through the patterns of habitual unsatisfactoriness. (All attempts to reduce Buddhism to a descriptive psychology or mentalistic philosophy must be likened to saying, for example, that Van Gogh's painting of sunflowers *is* just so many grams of cadmium yellow on a piece of canvas.)

We are presented, then, with the assertion that the best way to do something about the quality of our lives is to develop insight, to analyze those very situations in which we find ourselves. Various techniques have been elaborated in the course of time to help those who earnestly seek a way out of bewilderment and frustration. These methods are always intended as pointers, suggesting the possibility of taking a new look at one's predicament. They were elaborated and developed for the sole purpose of helping one to discern the difference between those modes of being which lead to further entanglement and misery and those which lead to increasing clarity—attunement to reality shorn of all fictive notions and convulsive emotivity.

To the extent that we develop insight, the experienced narrowness of meaning is severed and an attendant feeling of calm ensues. The most radical severance gives rise to the broadest expanse of experienced meaning, termed Buddha (Tibetan: sangs-rgyas).

Buddha does not refer to any person as such, but rather to that dynamic mode of being in which the most intense responsiveness possible is actualized. The possibility of severing one's habitually narrowed experiences was the Lord Buddha's proclamation of the Third Truth (nirodha, 'gog-pa).

The careful and systematic expansion of meaningful horizons is what is commonly termed the Path. The demonstration and teaching of this systematic expansion was the proclamation of the Fourth Truth (mārga, lam). These Four Truths constitute the core of the Buddha's message to his fellow human beings. A thoughtful and serious reflection on the implications of each of the Truths might constitute the decisive step in entering into the opening and deepening of experience.

Situational Techniques

There are, of course, many methods and techniques elaborated within the Buddhist tradition. What follows is a detailed presentation of one such technique, best regarded as a sort of 'sublime gimmick': sublime in the sense that to the extent one learns to focus with it, one's horizon of meaning naturally expands; gimmick in that the technique itself, and the terms used to describe its application, can nowhere be found to exist.

This 'gimmick' emphasizes the predominance of recurring motifs in our experience. Twelve characteristic motifs are emphasized. These twelve items are only pointers highlighting various features of our everyday situations; they can never be isolated, for 'they' are always already imbedded in the field-character of our experience.

The method under discussion is termed pratītya-samutpāda (Tibetan: rten-cing-'brel-bar-'byung-ba). In terms of its application it might be rendered as 'the characteristic features of situational patterning'. Its proper use produces heightened awareness about the workings of karma ('phrin-las) such that habit patterns can be penetrated and broken. By 'karma' we indicate the name given to the observed intimate relatedness which obtains between one situation and another. It has a two-fold aspect, applying equally to (1) that stream of patterning (saṁtana, rgyun) which we experience as ourselves, and (2) the entire range of meaningful encounters that we experience as our world.

There is an important attitudinal assumption regulating the potency of this method. As one gains enough insight into one's lived situation one comes to realize (or at least strongly suspect) its ever-recurrent unsatisfactoriness. This realization should not be a morbid fixation manifesting as melancholic behavior. It should induce the desire to penetrate more deeply into the causes and conditions of one's life. This desire might be termed a healthy attitude and should be brought to mind whenever one finds oneself slipping into unhealthy attitudes characterized by (1) generating unanswerable questions ("What is the meaning of my life?" etc.) or (2) fixation on unsatisfactoriness (existential despair, morbidity, etc.).

After a healthy attitude has been established, one should call to mind the Three Marks of Conditioned Existence (trilakṣaṇa, mtshan-nyid-gsum) which can be applied to every motif given by the method. The Three Marks are:

1. Unsatisfactoriness (duḥkha, sdug-bsngal), meaning the motifs indicated are not inherently desirable.

2. Non-entitativeness (anātman, bdag-med), meaning one motif cannot be found to exist in isolation from the other eleven: Each motif is relational in structure and arises in conjunction with the others.

3. Transitoriness (anitya, mi-rtag-pa), meaning the cognized existence of these motifs is momentary, consisting of (a) an arising, (b) a fleeting stabilization, and (c) a falling away or breaking up.

Twelve Motifs

The term pratītyasamutpāda indicates dependence (pratītya) upon conditions which are variously originated (samutpāda), and so is often translated simply as dependent origination. It avoids the two interpretative extremes of eternalism and nihilism. Eternalism, in this context, is the false inference that because there is an observed regularity of patterning to our experience, there must be an active agent or 'mover' to that pattern. Nihilism, on the other hand, is the doctrine of those who dispute the claim of there being a regularity of patterning, or else maintain that all action is fruitless because it is predetermined by fate.

The Lord Buddha taught that our experience is not determined by fate, but by conditions that can be known and changed. The conditional relation is intrinsically causal. That is, there is nothing external to the unfolding situation in which I now find myself. The karmic law of this unfolding is the intrinsic and (to those who look carefully) compulsive patterning of events.

Having briefly characterized the general meaning of the term, we now move to a discussion of each of the twelve motifs.

1. *avidyā, ma-rig-pa* This is usually rendered as 'ignorance'. It refers to the condition of bewilderment and confusion due to a wrong assessment of reality. As the first of the twelve motifs, it might lend itself to being seen as the starting point or cause of worldly existence. It is not a cosmogenic principle or metaphysical cause but simply the condition under which our present life develops. Perhaps it is best imagined as a continuous gradient characterizing not so much a particular state of being, but the quality or direction of situational patterning, experienced as a 'falling away from' the modality of pristine awareness. It involves a dimming of clarity and a progressive enmeshing into structures of this-and-that.

2. *saṁskāra, 'du-byed* This motif refers to the impulse accumulation or energetic activity which always accompanies the direction of situational patterning characterized by the first motif. This activity manifests through the body, speech, and mind as structuring forces of our being-in-the-world. It forms the basis of our character, our personal karmic patterning.

3. *vijñāna, rnam-par-shes-pa* The next motif, vijñāna, refers to the partially structured consciousness that follows from the action of saṁskāra. It indicates the molding of that energetic activity into a kind of frozen energy, a partial psy-

The Wheel of Life (bhavacakra) represents the cyclic nature of pratītya-samutpāda, shown in the outer circle, beginning in the upper right with the blind man carrying a stick (ignorance). The six realms of existence are represented in the inner circle, and the three root defilements (lust, hatred, and ignorance) in the center.

chic complex. It is pictured as having a twofold function: the cognition of objects that arise in the field of our awareness and a structured stream that is being continually fed from the reservoir of energetic activity. The interplay between saṁskāra and vijñāna is seen as accounting for all the experiential data associated with the psychological notion of the unconscious, including memory, dreams, and the eruption of emotive complexes.

4. *nāma-rūpa, ming-gzugs* Vijñāna is never found by itself. It has a flashing, grasping quality, jumping from sense objects to objects of imagination quite quickly. It can as easily crystallize and polarize into material forms, called rūpa, as into mental functions, called nāma.

Nāma refers to three components of mental functioning. There is the sensation or tone-awareness of a mental situation. There is also an ideational or labeling function. And finally there is the component of dispositional orientation, the 'mood-energy' we bring to a situation.

Rūpa refers to the four dynamic structuring operations of solidity, cohesion, heat, and motility. They are represented by the elemental symbols of earth, water, fire, and air. The operation of these elemental modes goes to make up what we experience as our physical world, including our body. Rūpa embraces the static aspects of embodiment such as cellular, tissue, and organ structures, as well as the dynamic aspect of body metabolism—electro-physiological pathways, membrane transport, etc. As a collective term, nāma-rūpa indicates the close working of bodily and mental functioning.

5. *ṣaḍāyatana, skye-mched-drug* The close working of bodily and mental functioning is further differentiated into the six-fold bases of awareness. These 'bases' (skye-mched) are to be pictured as furthering (mched) the birth (skye) or arising of all sensations which make up our experience. The

bases are grouped into internal (ādhyātmika, nang) and external (bāhya, phyi) supports.

The internal grouping refers to the integration of five sensory capabilities (eye, ear, nose, tongue, body) and a sixth capability, termed non-sensuous or mental, which refers to the capability of all acts of memory, imagination, visualization, etc. These internal bases are not to be confused with the corresponding physical organs, which as such are capable of being anatomically dissected. They are simply loci of sensitivity structured such that there arises the experience of seeing, hearing, etc.

The six external bases, which always work in conjunction with the corresponding internal base, refer to the six types of possible object awareness. These bases are the means by which the differentiated aspects, which are fleeting stabilizations in the field character of our awareness, stand out long enough to be appropriated as this-or-that specific object. The external and internal bases should be pictured as working together in pairs. In any given moment there is the twofold working of a particular modality of awareness (eye-sensitivity and color-forms, ear-sensitivity and sounds, etc.).

6. *sparśa, reg-pa* The next motif refers to the contact or rapport between the internal and external āyatana. This contact gives rise to impressions of tone corresponding to the particular mode of sensing that has been activated.

7. *vedanā, tshor-ba* This motif points to the six types of tone-awareness, which result from the contact of the āyatana. It expresses the fact that the experience of seeing— its feeling tone—is quite distinct from that of hearing or smelling. Each modality is experientially separable on the basis of (a) the *place* of sensitivity (internal base), (b) the corresponding *structure* of its field (external base), (c) the manner of articulation or relatedness between (a) and (b), termed rapport, and (d) the resulting distinctive tone.

8. *tṛṣṇā, sred-pa* Following rather automatically and habitually upon the arising of tone-awareness is a corresponding craving or thirst for that which has been experienced. Many types of craving or attachment may ensue, depending on (a) which of the six modalities has been activated, and (b) which of the three so-called 'motivations' it has been joined to.

The motivation of sensual gratification (kāma-tṛṣṇā) is perhaps the most common. It results in simple attachment to whatever arises in one's field of awareness. It is not an overt appropriation, one that we consciously activate. It refers rather to the habitual structuring of experience such that one is compulsively caught up in one situation after another through a process of identification and clinging.

One can also be motivated with regard to the desire for 'eternals' (bhava-tṛṣṇā). It is the habitual structuring of any sensory impression, any momentary awareness, such that it might be the occasion for securing an eternal realm of peace and contentment.

Finally there is the annihilatory motivation (vibhava-tṛṣṇā). It is the automatic structuring of experience such that any sensory activation might be the cause of a compulsive thirst to annihilate and destroy. What is commonly regarded as psychopathic behavior might be linked particularly with this type of motivation.

All three of these possible motivations, it should be remembered, are encompassed within the motif of craving. As such all of them go into structuring the responsiveness of normal human beings.

9. *upādāna, len-pa* The very nature of craving tends to result in a firm grasping or overt clinging (upādāna). An analogy is commonly used to point up the differences between the motifs of craving and firm grasping: Tṛṣṇā is that which remains unachieved, like a thief groping for goods in

the dark. Upādāna, however, is the fruition of this groping, when the thief finally lays hands on the object of searching.

10. *bhava, srid-pa*   Once the direction of situational patterning has proceeded to the point of overt clinging, a process of becoming, termed bhava, is initiated. It refers to the new formation of karmic tendencies. It differs from saṁskāra in its temporal reference. Saṁskāra refers to tendencies from past situational patternings (lives) which act on the present situation. Bhava, however, refers to the creation of new habits and tendencies which will have their fruition in future experiences.

11. *jāti, skye-ba*   This motif refers to the fruition of the last motif. It is the first appearance of new patternings, which may be seen in two ways. It refers to being-in-a-new-situation. It also refers to that which finds itself in a new situation. In a psycho-biological model, jāti refers to the birth or emergence of a newborn being, appearing, according to the specific history of patterning, in one of six 'lifestyles'. These lifestyles indicate the general character of experience. They are symbolized by the terms gods, titans, hungry ghosts, animals, denizens of hell, and human. These embrace all the general ways of being-in-a-situation.

12. *jarā-maraṇa, rga-shi*   Once a new situation or a new being has emerged, it is inevitable that the conditions which brought about its appearance will change. This, the last of the twelve motifs, points to the inevitability of decay and death. Decay affects all structures, which are but fleeting stabilizations fed by the energy flow of habitual patterning. When the cessation of the continuity of experience occurs, we speak of death. It is the total breakdown and dissolution of experience and experiencer.

The process of disintegration, destructuring, and entropic scattering yields a nexus of vibratory murkiness which is the condition of avidyā, the first motif. Thus the entire structure of patterning feeds back on itself, and is often pictured as a circle of twelve sections, called the Wheel of Life (bhava-cakra, srid-pa'i-'khor-lo).

Applications

There are many possible ways of using this scheme. Only a few will be suggested. For example, there are several ways to move from one motif to another:

The forward order, from (1) to (2) and so on, through (12), is recommended for those who are deluded about the conditions or origin of the manifold factors of experience. Careful attention to the logic of forward movement should, with practice, yield a clearer understanding.

The reverse order of movement is recommended for those who have as their specific concern or confusion the problem of birth, decay and death. Starting from a contemplation of these motifs, one would then move backwards through clinging, thirst, tone-awareness, contact, etc., gradually penetrating the connectedness and 'origin' of each motif.

One can also start from the middle (8) and proceed in reverse order up to (1). This is meant as an exercise for penetrating into situations of past patterning so as to account for the present.

Starting from the middle (8) and proceeding to the last term (12) is for the purpose of penetrating into present conditions such that one might better understand the probable consequences in the future.

For those whose psychical make-up is dominated by speculative confusions (dṛṣṭi-carita), contemplation of motifs (1) through (7) is sufficient, showing the unbroken continuity of causes and conditions.

For those dominated by attractions towards worldly things (tṛṣṇā-carita), contemplation of motifs (8) through

(12) is recommended. It counteracts the belief in permanence (śāśvata-dṛṣṭi) by showing the inevitability of decay and death.

These motifs may be regarded as occurring simultaneously or in temporal succession. In the latter case the motifs (1) and (2) represent the past, (3) through (10) the present, and (11) and (12) the future.

As mentioned before, the entire scheme is a representation of the direction of patterning, which, as the predominant modality of responsiveness, is marked by suffering, frustration, and unhappiness. These motifs are compulsively linked together, but are capable of being broken.

Of these twelve motifs, avidyā (1), tṛṣṇā (8), and upādāna (9) represent the predominance of bewildering emotivity (kleśa). Saṃskāra and bhava represent the predominance of consequent action patterning (karma). The seven remaining motifs provide the continuing ground of unsatisfactoriness (duḥkha). Emotivity, compulsive actions, and unsatisfactoriness are pictured as the three legs of the tripod called samsara. The removal, through penetrating insight (prajñā), of any one leg is sufficient to topple the entire structure.

This method, and the techniques of application briefly indicated above, are only meant as suggestions. As an analysis of the causes of unsatisfactoriness, it is vulnerable to being wrongly assessed as a conceptual scheme. Like all methods of the Buddha's teaching, it was elaborated to help gain a new perspective. Unless seriously used, it is nothing but an intellectual plaything to be fitted into our already burgeoning files of interesting data.

How to Meditate

Even a small concept—one moment's negative thought—can completely change and turn you around. So be very mindful and careful.

The traditional way to start instruction in meditation is that the teacher points out the various teachings through words and encourages the student to follow in that direction, so that the student can gradually reach the same understanding and experience as the teacher. In other words, the teacher knows better than the student: The teacher has traveled a long distance, and now he can explain the map and direct the student, because through his experience he knows the territory well. "Walk this way, go in this direction, and then this will happen."

In this process, it is the student's role to follow the map exactly; to go where he is led. If that does not happen, then the experience or realization will not come. So if there are no results, there are various possibilities: The teaching is wrong, the teacher is wrong, the map or guidance is not accurate, or something in the student is not prepared to follow the instructions.

But the only way to find out is by trying. The instructions or guidelines are only ideas, but you have to use these ideas in order to understand accurately and to follow the path. This is a kind of transmission. When you become enlightened, there is no more transmitting anything, but before that there is need of transmission. First there must be solid understanding; then when you fully understand, you will know that there is really nothing to understand.

We are still talking on the level of concepts and ideas. But the ideas may have a certain magnetism that leads toward a kind of understanding. And that understanding itself in a way becomes illuminated. At that time there is silence: There is no need to question, no need to answer, no need to conceptualize. There is nothing to be done. That is why we say, "There's nothing to do, nothing to understand."

Language is mostly interpretation, and interpretation can take us up to a certain point, but it is really only an instrument to aid understanding. The same is true for all ideas, all concepts, all theories. The experience itself is beyond language, beyond interpretation, beyond concepts. At that time of direct experience, you may develop a very special kind of certainty: You are sure, because there is no longer any self-deception.

In the beginning, meditation is always an idea: Something to do, some place to reach, something to get, something that is supposed to happen. These are just mental ideas, mental projections. It is important to recognize that it is very hard to understand meditation intellectually. We may give certain simple instructions, we may say 'how' to meditate, and everybody believes that that is meditation. Then the challenge becomes how to follow these instructions, how to 'do' meditation. But the more you experience and understand your own mind directly, the easier meditation becomes.

As long as you do not examine your own mind, you will have a hard time meditating, because meditation is not yet a part of you. It is somewhere else, something else, a particular idea. If this idea of something separate is perpetuated, we can never contact meditation. So first we must go through the ego's understanding of meditation, go through our concepts about meditation, go through our clinging and grasping meditation as a goal or as something that will give us what we want.

For some people, this may not be a difficulty at all. If you say "Go," they go. If you say, "Walk," they walk. They are completely ready, and they can just contact the meditative state directly. But other people are not ready to hear this. Perhaps they are not sensitive at a certain level, or they do not want to contact the meditative state badly enough. For these people the teachings are available, but they are not accessible. It is not really a matter of effort. The only difference is that some people seem to have a natural ability to understand this easily. You may read books every day, you may practice many exercises, and it still does not help that much. The harder you try, the more obstacles arise.

If you suspect that this is your situation, ask what it is that you know and what you do not know. You may understand basically how to meditate. But you have to understand from inside, within awareness, within your own concepts, within your natural state. Then you do not need to talk or question; you do not need to learn complicated theories.

As long as you want something more, as long as you are not sure, then you have to find teachers or teachings that can help you dissolve your questioning and searching. But the day you are absolutely sure there is nothing to be questioned and nothing to be learned, then that is it. There is no more running after anything outside yourself any more.

At that time it will be difficult to fool yourself, because you can set up all kinds of tests to see if you still have negative emotions, or anger, or ego. You can see whether you are still caught up in grasping and in concepts. Then you will know the direction in which you need to grow.

In terms of practice, this way of practicing does not involve a fixed object. Within the meditation, whatever you want, you can do. But you have to test yourself. You have to test your thoughts, your emotions, your own experience. How is it? Just cut through your hesitations and do it.

Sometimes—a certain time, or a certain day—you just naturally find yourself in the meditative state. There is no problem; meditation just comes. At that time, meditation is really working well, and you do not need any additional teaching. Meditation itself takes care of you, and through meditation you become your own teacher or master. Ultimately there is no higher teacher than you yourself. But how can you teach? What qualifications do you need? You have to be aware, open, and watchful. Then you are ready to teach yourself.

The Buddha always said, "My teaching is alive." So daily living becomes the teaching, becomes the test. That means that when you get up in the morning, you have to deal with the morning, with very practical matters. The practice is not only when you are sitting in meditation, but in everything. The raw material is our flesh, our breath, our environment, and what needs to be done. We may have some idea of enlightenment, or heaven, or certain very beautiful samādhis, but even these are not 'somewhere else'. These things all belong within the intrinsic nature of the mind.

If these things are meaningful to you, then from time to time you need to remind yourself of them. Sometimes you may find some other practice that works well for you. Good, take it! If something is not working well, then possibly your head is not communicating with your heart, or it is possible that you are not following the instructions accurately or precisely. So if there is something lacking, you can check and maybe change it, or try to do things differently. On the other hand, if something works, continue to develop it. Whatever happens, do not give up.

Sometimes you might give in just a little, and then many distractions come and you get lost. Perhaps other people try to change your ideas. "Forget it!" they say. "Nothing happens in meditation; there is never any progress." Or you may say to yourself, "This is just taking time and wasting my energy, and nothing is happening anyway." Then other conflicts come, and in the end you give up before there has been any progress. Even a small concept—one moment's negative thought—can completely change and turn you around. So be very mindful and careful.

Sustaining your faith and your trust is one of the most important parts of developing a spiritual life. Everybody can be fascinated or interested for a short period of time or for a couple of years, but particularly in this time of the Kāli Yuga, if you can sustain and learn to develop your awareness, this is one of the most useful and positive things you can do. The more complicated and conflicting the world and society become, the more difficult it is to survive spiritually—to survive internally—because everything is against you, luring you away from meditation and inner calm, from your own sense of inner guidance and wisdom. So be very aware and careful, and develop mindfulness in each activity and in each situation.

Each moment has the potential to be destructive to you, internally and externally. So knowing that the destruction is there, you have to completely transform it. Whatever the situation or emotion or samsaric activity, you are not controlled by it; you are 'above' it.

You can control your own life once you realize that mind itself is empty. Mind is awareness, and it manifests all these existent forms from nothing. When you have really and completely understood this, then no situation is too difficult. Even though you may be very frustrated in dealing with your emotions, if you look at them in the same moment that you are having the difficulty, it is possible to see that they are just manifesting from nothing. There is nothing particularly solid there. So you can liberate yourself from difficult situations through your own strength and knowledge, your own understanding.

The real problem is not the imagined difficulty or obstacle, but how you look at it, how you understand your situation. Once you deeply understand your mind's nature and see it as empty, it is easy to gain perspective on the daily situations of life and to have great inner strength that lets you handle problems as they arise.

Most of the time we believe that the mind is concrete, with a specific shape and color. We believe that the mind 'has' senses, and that some 'thing' is there. So work first with this mistaken view. Realize that the mind is absolutely empty, completely open. Once that is established, then gradually awareness is developed. And the more awareness develops, the more you can open to an experience that has the nature of enlightened mind.

Analyzing the
Judging Mind

Do we really want to apply explanations and theories to questions about our nature as human beings?

To understand the Dharma, to really experience its essence, is to have clear insight into the nature of one's self and the relation of that self to the world. The Buddhist tradition is rich in methods for achieving this insight. Yogic practices, devotional sādhanas, philosophical studies, and the use of mantra, visualizations, art, and music are all used, and all have their particular value.

There are many people concerned with understanding themselves who are interested in the *outcome* of such practices, but not in doing the practices themselves. In some cases, this is due to a bias in favor of a particular style of thinking, considered logical or rational. Other ways of knowing are considered suspect or even simply invalid. They are unverifiable and unscientific.

For some such people, rational inquiry into the status of the self may prove rewarding. This inquiry would consist of a process of analysis guided and directed by a certain purpose, yet never departing from what is immediately and concretely given. There are many examples of such analysis in the Buddhist tradition. Here we can perhaps suggest the flavor of such an analysis, leaving it to the reader to explore in more detail.

We start with the simple question, "Who am I?" This question should be repeated and considered, seriously and intensely, again and again. Whatever answers come need to be challenged: Are they really answers? What do they mean?

Whatever answers we give, there is the process of analyzing or judging that leads to the answer. Instead of staying with the answers, we can turn to this process of judging. Who has made this judgment? And, in the moment that we consider this question, we can ask, "Who is analyzing or judging this judgment?"

At this point it seems that we will fall into an infinite regress, for we can never get hold of the one who is currently engaged in judging without making a new judgment. Instead, we can ask how the judgments come about. What is their nature and how do they work? This is not a theoretical inquiry, and answers given in terms of concepts—consciousness, recognition, discrimination, etc.—need to be grounded in the specific elements of our experience. An answer that depends on definitions will not meet the test of direct experience. In each case, we can ask what such concepts depend on, and how and why they arise as they do.

Suppose we give an answer in terms of our personality, memories, ideas, etc. The same questions are still pertinent. What accounts for the particular disposition that is 'me'? What causes it to arise, to take the form it does? Does it reside in thought, or in consciousness? How is it caused? If it is not caused, how can it hold a position, or provide a basis for experience or judgment? Again and again we must ask how, what, and why. Even more fundamentally, we can ask: "How do you know that?"

At this point certain objections may be raised. For instance, it may seem perfectly obvious that we cannot explain the elements of our experience by an appeal to those elements; that this would require a theory that operates at a different level. Or we may argue that we cannot account for the elements of experience because we *are* those elements; or else that our *sense* of self results from the same generative agencies (for example, the brain) as those elements. Each of these views leads to the claim that we cannot examine and experience the elements of awareness (including 'the self') directly.

Such approaches, however, seem to set unduly restrictive limits on the analysis we are attempting, prejudging what might be found. The first view makes key assumptions about what counts as an explanation; the second makes equally fundamental assumptions about what 'we' are (for example, that 'we' can be reduced to a set of physiological functions). Both can be subjected to the same kind of challenging inquiry that we are attempting to set in motion here and now.

Any theory is just that: tentative and limited; any explanation is a reconstruction or representation of what experience presents. The point here is not to refute a particular position, but to clear the way for access to direct perception that would otherwise be barred. Do we really want to apply explanations and theories to questions about our own nature as human beings? Accurate and appropriate as such answers may be within certain domains and for certain purposes, are we willing to use them to determine what we are and what we can be? Could it be that taking this approach really only sidesteps the most fundamental issue?

If we do not let our inquiry be halted by 'solutions' that are perhaps better suited to other kinds of investigations, but instead continue with our questioning, we may find that what each of us calls 'my self' is perhaps better seen as the outcome of uncritical identification with many layers and levels of sense impressions, feeling tones, sensory data, and reactions. When we fail to notice that we are accepting and identifying in this way, we may impose limits on ourselves that are unnecessary and even harmful. Clinging to the results of this identification, protecting and defending structures that may well be unstable and ultimately indefensible, we generate tension and misery.

A more careful inquiry might give us a new place to stand, a vantage point from which everything looked very different. Concentrating on the activity of judging, probing its causes and conditions, its nature and manner of operations, we go deeper into aspects of the mind that are ever present but seldom explored. Gradually we may begin to see the judging activity of mind to be somewhat insubstantial and dreamlike. The result may be that the mind surrenders and opens, leading to something quite unexpected, a kind of liberation from a bondage we did not even recognize.

This experience of liberation will not occur if the analysis is conducted as a philosophical game or pastime. Instead, we must plunge into it, holding nothing back. But this is exactly where we usually draw back. We are afraid of making this effort, afraid of the possibility of real transcendence, of giving up something we hold most precious. Afraid that we might 'go crazy' or else 'do something crazy', we stay bound to ordinary mind, with all its limitations and delusions.

As a way of gaining confidence, we might remind ourselves that enlightenment does not consist in being spaced out. The Lord Buddha, who encouraged minute and thorough-going analysis of the self, was not a careless or irresponsible person, and he would not have recommended a style of inquiry that disorients people or makes them unfit to live life fully and well.

The confusion, pain, and fear that we may feel when our ordinary world and ordinary structures are called into question are a mirror for the confusion, pain, and fear that we feel again and again within those structures. Ultimately, it seems there is no solution except to face our fears at their source. The Buddha taught that there is actually nothing to fear: that the source of our fear and our pain is a lack of understanding that is basic to our present condition but is also capable of being remedied.

We can test this possibility for ourselves by playing the game of samsara against itself. What happens if we give the mind a chance to generate more fictions, freely and without limits, with the only condition being that we are ready to see each fiction as just that? What will we lose? Could it be that we will only lose the basic fear that tries to prevent us from being free?

In one way, we can offer our fearful mind some reassurance. Analysis can offer only the beginning of clear vision. If we do not aspire to perfect realization (whether we call it Buddha nature, omniscience, or anything else), we are perfectly safe. The practice cannot take us where we do not want to go.

In the beginning, our goal can be more modest. Let us strive for self-knowledge—how could this be threatening? Perhaps on the psychological level there are things about ourselves that we would rather not know, but now we are talking about something deeper. Once we have started questioning, we are still free to decide what is really valuable to us. Perhaps we will discover aspects of ourselves that we want to preserve unaltered. If that is the outcome, fine and good. As long as we are willing to go where our questioning leads us, we do not need to fear that we will arrive at some undesired place, a kind of black hole, only to find that there is no way to retrace our steps.

The Buddha was not concerned with allowing us to have novel kinds of experience, nor did he wish to develop propositions and theories that more or less fit the data. He was concerned with absolute conviction. What is our nature as human beings? What are our possibilities? What are our limits, and are those limits final?

The answer to those questions does not arise from theories. Knowledge that is certain, that cannot be separated from being, grows out of a synthesis of insight and action, and manifests as a new way of being. Searching for the self without straying from the self, starting with analysis, committed to inquiry, we can learn who we are. Why would we ever voluntarily accept anything less?

Mind and Feelings

*In its true state, mind is naked, immaculate,
not made of anything, being of the Voidness,
clear, vacuous, without duality, transparent,
timeless, uncompounded, unimpeded, colorless,
not realizable as a separate thing, but as the
unity of all things, yet not composed of them,
of one taste, and transcendent over differentiation.*

Padmasambhava

It is very important that as human beings we have feelings. Sometimes it is difficult for us to understand our own mind or consciousness, but the feelings of our mind and body are familiar to us and are always available.

In general, there are three types of feelings. The first are positive: happy, joyful, balanced. The second are negative: irritated, frustrated, or restless, a kind of basic discomfort. The third are neither positive nor negative, but neutral and dull: Nothing is happening.

In our lives it is important to develop positive feelings. Normally, feelings divide the mind: This is a good feeling, this is a bad feeling. Like mail which goes to many different countries, the mind distributes our thoughts and feelings in different directions. This means that feelings generally control us. We say that we follow our feelings, but this does not give the whole picture: Pulled by our feelings this way and that, we are like blind men crossing a busy street.

Once feelings take over in this way, we have little choice as to whether the feelings we experience will be positive. But if we develop the mind, we can take charge, making sure that we cultivate positive feelings, examining our mental attitudes to see that they develop in a positive way. If the mind is clear, the negative residues and ongoing emotional turbulence of each day do not need to disrupt that clarity; instead, they can be used to strengthen a balanced, positive attitude. But how can we learn to make use of each situation in this way?

Just where is this mind that we want to develop? We tend to think of whatever we can name as having a particular form, but mind has no form. In each immediate experience, the mind presents itself more as energy.

We might say that the mind is like empty space that can adopt or support many different forms. Without space, we cannot make shape, color, or form. Without space, nothing can exist. So mind as space is a continuum that is not solid. Mind in its emptiness, mind-nature, is like empty light, or like a crystal that reflects the color and shape of all things. In its spaciousness, mind is like the ocean.

If mind is like space, then by nature mind has no position, no characteristics. Mind is not a thing or substance; it has no form, no color, no beginning. Mind does not go anywhere; it does not belong to anyone, it is not 'a' mind, or 'the mind'. It is not something individual, and it has no parents.

How does this empty mind become linked to our very individual reactions and our personal identity? How is it that we become conditioned? Actually, it is our ego or self-image that determines our conditioning. Like carpenters working with wood, we make use of mind to shape our individual identity. We draw on the creative power or energy of mind, which arises through its emptiness, but we do this in a way that moves toward limitation. We label or name the ways that mind appears, and this results in thoughts, perceptions, and concepts. In this way we continue to develop samsara, which evolves in accord with this dynamic. The feelings that we have, whether positive, negative, or neutral, arise in accord with this conditioning, without our having any control over the process.

The more we come to understand what mind truly is, the more rapidly our conception of mind changes, and the more new possibilities open. At first we may think we understand mind, but we are only operating on the basis of concepts and labels that arise 'within' mind. Later, our concepts and labels change, and while this is still happening within mind, something has begun to shift.

To take advantage of the energy and knowing that this shift makes available, we must look at the mind at an experiential level. We can ask questions that do not call for scientific answers, but that invite us to involve ourselves with the answers at the immediate, practical level. If the mind has substance, should we not have some 'from', some origin? If we say mind 'exists' a certain way, then what does this mean about where we come from or how our experience arises? We want to know these answers not in a purely intellectual way, just in our heads, but according to how we actually feel.

Regarding feelings, we may ask whether feelings are possible without mind. It seems that all feelings arise from the mind. Then can we at the same time deny mind and accept feelings? Can we say they are the same?

We do not need a laboratory to test these questions. Our laboratory is here within us, in our feelings and in our own capacity to investigate. By learning to question each experience, we can make use of each situation, each emotional disturbance. As we bring clarity to our feelings, they no longer control us. Instead, they guide us to the nature of mind, and teach us who and what we are.

The Self-Image

A magic spell, a dream, a gleam before the eyes,
A reflection, lightning, an echo, a rainbow,
Moonlight upon water, cloud-land, dimness
Before the eyes, fog, and apparitions,
These are the twelve similes of the phenomenal.

Nāropa

A human being *is* the embodiment of his or her consciousness. In other words, what it is to be a human being is the same physically as it is mentally. There is no difference. What a person thinks and feels and how that person acts reflect the present state of consciousness.

We may say that a person is really functioning properly as a human being when his consciousness is well-balanced. If he is out of balance or has specific problems, such as mental or physical blockages, these difficulties can be seen on the physical level. A person's characteristic behavior patterns—his obsessions, his dullness, his unhappiness, or his feelings of great fulfillment—are all manifested on the physical level as well.

But the physical level is not all. If we observe our constant play of thoughts and ideas, we will find that we have many thoughts and many conceptions about who or what we are. Our thoughts are so involved with a self-image! We expect ourselves to behave in certain ways. We see ourselves sitting in a certain way, or wearing certain kinds of clothes, or talking in a certain manner. All these are expressions of individual characteristics that take on a separate form—a 'personality' that is different from who we actually are.

Recognizing the Self-Image

The self-image directly represents our level of consciousness. First, we create thoughts or thought-models that feed our consciousness. At once our consciousness becomes involved in a different world that comes into being as our thoughts form. This is the world of our self-image. Although we could present more philosophically the various levels at which the self-image operates, this is basically what the self-image is.

Self-image is interesting because when we examine it, it does not show itself. We think and talk as if we could actually touch or see our self-image, but this self-image cannot be pinpointed as anything. Bound to thoughts, it disperses; it is nothing. True, you may have concepts about a certain self-image you have at a particular time, but there is no *one* particular self-image that outlasts any conceptions you may have about it.

It is important to understand that there are actually two separate qualities or factors at work in experience: the self, or 'me' or 'I', and the self-image. The 'me' or 'I' is involved with life in a multitude of ways: It experiences and feels and sees things in a way which is very alive, very immediate. This is the operation of the five skandhas or elements that make up the human being. But apart from these there is an additional force which is the self-image. When the 'I' becomes imbued with the self-image, the person is not 'really' himself. He is acting as if he were some other person.

For example, through the operation of self-image you may feel tremendously shy, or shameful, embarrassed or guilty. You may feel afraid, or that your life is in danger, or that you are dissatisfied. At these times the 'I' is overcome with a very vivid, very alive sensation that is really only the activation of the self-image.

To explore the operation of self-image, we can think, examine, and meditate, making very clear to ourselves what kind of status we are giving to this self-image. Let us say you are watching your thoughts and emotions during some tremendous disturbance, some great sadness. Your mind is very agitated. At these times you might be able to observe that you are not actually the person who is experiencing this emotional state or feeling the pain. You are not the one creating those disturbances. They are being created through the operation of your self-image.

Sometimes this is hard to see because you are so involved with the self-image. After all, you have created it throughout your life. But exactly during such particularly painful disturbances, you have the opportunity to step back and actually see the core of your self-image. For instance, when certain energies develop—a trembling or volcanic sort of consciousness, or a feeling of fear, or anger, or tightness—what is creating this holding-strength is the self-image. Just like the self-image, this holding-strength does not really exist. True, the actual feeling is there, but its holding-power will be completely lost as soon as you have lost your interest in feeding the self-image. At that time you can have a totally different experience than what you had thought was possible in the previous moment, when the pain seemed so real and solid.

It is so easy to let the self-image perpetuate itself, so that it dominates your whole life and creates an unbalanced state of affairs. In this way you become a prisoner, and at some level you feel that you are inside a cage. But you accept this blockage. In fact, some people don't really like to act in different ways, even if the present situation invites a new response. Such a person almost always moves in predictable ways. He could act in different ways, he could initiate different gestures, but he is like a sick man, and somehow the energy is lacking. On the physical or psychological level, this may manifest as a tightness or restrictiveness. Such a person does not want to open up—either to the situation or to other people's gestures or expressions.

The self-image is like a disease that is attached to the person: it is fixed to him, so that he can act only in certain specific ways, even if the situation calls for and even requires something different. The outcome is failure and a sense of frustration and loss.

How can we involve ourselves less with our self-image and make ourselves more flexible? Until we start investigating self-image through thinking, analysis, and meditation, it is quite difficult to change, for we are completely identified with the self-image. Since we do not realize the difference between our self-image and our self, we do not have an access-gate or point of departure. But if we can recognize just some small difference between self and self-image, this 'I' or 'me' that we accept, we can then see which part is the self-image.

Once we have recognized the self-image, we will see that it is neither flexible nor lucid. It is like a yak's horn, hard, restricted and narrow. The self-image does not allow anything to enter other than its own rigid constructions. It does not accept what might be. Can we see this? Unless we actually recognize the self-image for what it is, it is difficult for us to willingly admit that these sorts of things are actually happening to us.

Looking at Self-Image

In order to make ourselves more flexible, we must first learn to recognize this self-image. *It is not you.* All this is a very big subject, but here we are talking about self-image in a simple, practical way. For example, we may experience an emotional disturbance, or have deep physical feelings of dissatisfaction. Perhaps it is a sexual problem. Whatever the cause, many people have times when they feel frustrated. They feel energy blockages. This may be due to a great deal of fantasizing which creates an image, an idea, which can never be experienced in reality.

When you imagine or think about it, such thoughts and feelings are almost visible. They hold tremendous energy, but it is frustration-energy. Thus, it may be that this energy manifests in a negative form. The individual actually feels as if his energy is being drawn away, as if he is drowning in his own sorrow. The feeling may be completely hopeless—a feeling of desperation. If this situation intensifies, the emotions feel very thick, dense, dark and confused.

The energy of frustration causes the person to want to cry, but he does not know why. He has no reasons or explanations for this unhappy state. Energy is drawn up, then it collapses completely. There is no life, no light, no positive feelings. There may well be many fantasies, dreams and expectations, but none of these things happen. Nothing comes alive. All that he experiences is the expression of what he would like to have happen, and this just makes matters worse.

Now these feelings have a self-fulfilling effect: They cause the individual to remain in his own realm, his own world. This is the expression of self-image: a view that proclaims its own reality and keeps us stuck there. But it is exactly the strength of this holding-power that offers a way out. If we can let go of that energy, that holding-power, we can immediately separate from it. Instantly we feel different. How this comes about is not easy to explain in advance, but the experience speaks for itself. It leaves little doubt.

You can learn this awareness or looking, especially when you have obsessions or fantasies. At these times you can see the restrictive self-image and separate yourself from it. For example, suppose you do not have any good friends and you feel very lonely. You fantasize obsessively about wanting to be happy. Make your fantasy more vivid, more alive. You can almost see it, feel it, touch it. For instance, men do a lot of fantasizing about women's bodies, or about relationships with women, and the opposite is true for women. In this imagining, a person creates sensational feelings and generates much energy. You can feel that energy and vividly visualize it. Use this fresh energy to arouse your awareness. With this awareness, separate yourself from the image-making activity, and immediately look back at your situation.

To recognize this energy before it consumes you, you must develop an awareness that can look 'back' at the situation you have created, while 'you' are still 'in' it. At this time the energy-strength is felt very differently—it is like two different worlds, two different kinds of energies. When you step back, you can use this fresh energy to see the world of your involvement with the self-image.

Feeding the Self-Image

Caught up in the self-image, which is our own creation, we are trapped in an endless maze. As hard as we try, we will never find any satisfaction. This is because we are not feeding the right person, what we might call our 'real self'. Instead, we take whatever nourishment experience makes available and offer it to our self-image. The result can only be frustration.

When we eat physical food, we do not know exactly where the food goes. We know that it has combined with different substances in our body and has actually become a different substance—the original substance no longer exists. In the same way, when our thoughts and emotions feed our self-image, they become something different from what they might otherwise be. We have grown used to seeing them in their self-image form. But a whole different way of experiencing is possible.

There is a simple children's story that helps make this point. In Tibet, there are many groundhogs. In the wintertime, the bears like to eat the groundhogs, who hibernate underground. In the story, a bear digs around, finds a groundhog, hits it, and, thinking he has killed it, sets it aside for later. But the groundhog wakes up and runs away. Meanwhile the bear digs around again and finds another groundhog, hits it hard, and sets it aside. Again the same thing happens. This pattern repeats itself. The bear always wants to find *more*. So far, he has not even eaten the first groundhog, but he likes the idea of having many, so he keeps on digging. But meanwhile, all the groundhogs run away. In the end he has nothing left but the one he is holding.

In much this way, we keep trying to feed the desires of the self-image, without ever being satisfied. Caught in this cycle, we deny our self real satisfaction. It is true that sometimes we have a chance to find satisfaction in our feelings, in our immediate physical or mental needs. At those times, it is really *you yourself* that finds fulfillment—you feel open and clear and balanced. But most of the time we are working for the self-image. We can tell the difference easily once we know where to look, because when the self-image is in control, we always feel constricted.

The self-image can never feel satisfied, because there is nothing there. It is not connected to anything—it is nothing but our imagination. But this can be difficult to see clearly, because sometimes certain forms of our self-image can create definite sensations. Often it is very difficult for us to determine whether the sensations we have arise from 'us' or from our self-image. For instance, the sensations 'we' experience may go on to create enjoyable feelings of importance or goodness or security. Up to a certain point we are still in the domain of 'real' sensation. But the self-image, always trying to establish itself, has a strongly grasping nature. Holding on to the enjoyment and trying to make sensations permanent, it generates feelings of tightness. This grasping makes endless demands, so that we can never have enough.

Many of us have very creative minds and are able to visualize and fantasize very well. As a consequence, our self-image gets fed very regularly. Nonetheless, 'we' remain hungry. For example, you would like to have the experience you are creating in your mind. But you cannot have it because the energy you are creating is going to the self-image. You have certain physical needs and you want certain sensations fulfilled. This is the content of your thoughts and fantasies. But at the same time (and even if you get what you want) you feel deep dissatisfaction, as if there is a crying or a deep hurt within your subconsciousness. It is a very cloudy feeling, not happy or clear, a sort of moodiness inside that is like the atmosphere just before it rains. To change this pattern, you must get very clear on one point. Recognize the self-image, jump away from it and look at it—see that the self image is not 'you'.

Skillful Change

Many people go through life without ever changing certain facial expressions, gestures, or bodily postures. Because they are completely permeated by the self-image, the way they choose to live is always the same. But while it may be that we can recognize this in others, we need to see this rigidity in ourselves and work to change it.

One way to do this is to consciously challenge our patterns and old ways. For example, every time you think you are not happy say "I am happy." Say it strongly to yourself, even if your feelings seem to contradict you. Remember, it is your self-image that has these feelings, not 'you'.

Maybe it is true on a rational level that you have difficulties. Perhaps you do not have any money, or any friends, or a pleasant place to live, or satisfying work to do. Maybe you have fights with someone at work, or you discover that you have a serious illness. We can find all sorts of rational excuses for our difficulties and unhappiness. But you must forget the rational side. It is the self-image that relies on reasons to justify its responses.

Instead of relying on your good and valid reasons to explain your emotionality, just understand that you are not happy because your feelings are clouded. You feel uncertain: a dark, heavy feeling that dominates your whole being. You are not open. But just as fast as a fish can move in the water, you can instantly change to a happy attitude, a balanced attitude. Keep yourself there. Believe yourself. Be open to that positiveness. Even if the external conditions do not change right away, your whole inner situation can change at once. If you want to feel positive and have satisfaction, you can do it. Just be open and flexible. You have the choice.

At certain times you are definitely not happy. Certain things are occurring in a way you do not like. At such a time, mentally change your concept. Take a different perspective. When you do this, you will have a good opportunity to see the self-image in a true light—creating disturbances, insisting on its way, even if this means more unhappiness.

When you look back at the self-image, you may not want to believe you are that person. You may not really want to look, for you are afraid that you will see how dependent your consciousness and your reactions are on countless conditions. You will see that you are the victim of circumstances that you are creating. But the response is clear. When you understand that consciousness is really quite flexible, you will realize that what you see now does not have to trap you. In the next moment things can be different. As long as the self-image believes in its own stories, it will be rigid and unyielding, but as soon as we see it for what it is, the self-image becomes light and insubstantial, like a balloon that can just float away.

Mind in the Buddhist tradition is said to be diamond-like, and awareness is indestructible. But our consciousness in its present form does not manifest these qualities. To begin to make this transformation, it is important to develop flexibility in our consciousness. When we practice truly 'changing' our mind, we learn to accept experience in a simple way, not because we have to, but because there is no good reason not to. When you jump from one side of the experience to the other and then back again, or when you try to experience both at the same time, you will see there is no 'from' or 'to'. There is only awareness.

This experience is something like looking into a mirror and being in both 'places' at once. You can almost simultaneously feel two different atmospheres: one is constricted and constrained, the other is rich with a feeling of lightness, fullness, and wholeness.

You have the choice to stay in this fullness. This is being balanced, with everything interesting just as it is. In this circumstance, you feel no impediments, no distractions, no obstacles. You do not feel agitated or restless. You do not feel you have to go somewhere or get something, because at last you are feeding yourself directly, instantly. No longer under the control of the self-image, with its misguided and mistaken conceptual world, you are free.

Although this choice is ours, we have until now basically chosen to allow ourselves no choice. This is the role that the self-image forces us into and perpetuates. To challenge the reign of the self-image, we must be willing to experiment with certain ways or attitudes that may be different from ones we are familiar with. But this is not so difficult, because there is actually nothing substantial about us that needs to be changed. The actor is not solid. When we believe otherwise, we are accepting the claims of the self-image.

Even so, it happens that we do not want to change. We may be unwilling to see situations differently, to challenge the holding-strength of the self-image. But this is truly a sad state of affairs. We are addicted to suffering; we accept suffering as the truth of our lives and resist the invitation to challenge this addiction.

This pattern is deeply ingrained, and for most of us there will still be times when we must live through the difficulty of conforming to the self-image. But here too we have a choice. When we experience this difficulty fully; when we do not turn away from it or try to make it better, we are preparing the way to overthrow the self-image. At least then our suffering has a certain kind of value.

Because the self-image does not really exist, it is difficult to deal with or take hold of. In fact, you cannot exactly catch it at all. But at the same time, it dominates and controls us and makes us miserable.

Saying that we do not want to be miserable is not enough. Unless we come to some conclusions about what makes us suffer, we are only playing a game with ourselves. Since this is so, looking honestly and accepting what we see is the way to deal with self-image. Looking for knowledge and wisdom, seeking out a way of being that is mentally healthy and balanced, we force the self-image to show itself. Then it is up to us how we respond.

Friend, Teacher, and Guru

Your knowledge, realization, and all that you learn from daily experience can also be called your guru.

Until the last century or two, the attitude toward religion and spirituality here in the West seemed quite respectful. But as Westerners became more scientific in their outlook, the attitude toward spiritual teachers and also toward established churches changed. It began to seem that faith must be 'blind faith', and this was something that certain individuals were not ready to accept. Everything had to be proved intellectually and scientifically. Knowledge or understanding gained through faith or devotion was suspect; in fact, it was not knowledge at all. Clinging to religious beliefs came to be seen as a weakness.

All these difficulties were compounded when it came to the relationship between guru and disciple, student and teacher. Just as science made faith suspect, so the principles of democracy made any kind of authority suspect. Although few people in the West really had any sense of what the relationship between guru and student was all about, it seemed clear that the teacher was somehow above the student, and many people simply reject this kind of dependency relationship. The prevailing psychological perspective, which is closely linked to the basic 'democratic' orientation, viewed the inequality of the student-teacher relationship as suspect, tending toward the unhealthy.

On the other hand, the tradition of Vajrayāna Buddhism teaches that for the serious student a relationship to the teacher is vital. Of course, the teacher must be qualified: must have knowledge and must be ready to enter into a relationship of mutual trust and commitment. But if the teacher is truly able to serve this function, then faith, trust, devotion, and obedience toward the teacher are incredibly valuable. The teachings say that the most reliable teaching comes through the teacher; that even a person's internal understanding relies on the teacher's effort.

For some people who are more naturally attuned to spiritual or devotional practice, developing such a relationship of trust and devotion may not be so difficult, at least at first. But for others, it is simply not possible. It may be that such a commitment is too threatening to the ego's independence. First of all, it is uncomfortable to acknowledge that someone else knows something that you do not know. Second, you may lack confidence in your own knowledge, so that you fear being manipulated and making a fool of yourself. Finally, you may suspect that the knowledge the teacher has to offer you will prove to be painful or threatening to the self-image.

But perhaps this is too negative a way of describing it. For someone who is inspired by philosophy, psychology, or science, the path of devotion may seem unnecessary, even dangerous. You want guidance, but at the same time you want to be sure that you are learning by yourself. You do not want to accept knowledge without discovering it for yourself. All this has a very healthy aspect to it.

What is interesting is that on a deep level there may not be a real conflict between these two ways of proceeding. To see this, we must understand more clearly just why it is that the teacher or guru is said to be so important. In the Buddhist tradition, the key point is that the external teacher possesses or embodies the inspiration of the entire lineage of past teachers. This inspiration is itself a kind of understanding—of the Buddha, the Dharma, the deities, and the Bodhisattvas. And this understanding is transmitted directly to the student. It is like making prints from a wood block: Whatever is carved on the block will print out exactly the same each time. What remains the same, what gets transmitted from teacher to student, is inner realization.

Now, since the transmission has to do with inner realization, it might seem that the external guru himself is not the key to transmission. In one sense, this is true. Understood on a more inward level, 'guru' means 'internal awareness', or what is sometimes called your own Buddha nature. Your knowledge, your realization, and all that you learn from daily experience can also be called your guru.

But before we throw out the idea of an external guru, a 'real' teacher who is physically present, we need to ask how it is that this inner awareness can be activated. And here the role of the teacher once more takes on great importance. Inner realization does not readily come through your own actions. It requires the teacher's effort, a special effort that the teacher is able to make because he is the holder of the lineage. Because he has received the transmission of that lineage, he is now able to pass it on to the student.

This transmission can clarify to you that you *are* the Enlightened One. This happens not through intellectual insight, but through the guru's blessing, grace, or favor. This blessing has the power to 'charge' you with a kind of electricity, so that in your being you become like light. This is the power of the relationship between teacher and student.

Still, it is not that the teacher possesses something that the student must obtain. Exactly the same kind of power can flow as soon as the mind orients itself in a certain way. Surrender, devotion, openness, love, and compassion develop a deep serenity that is the basis for transformation. Seen in this light, the teacher—the one who is there to present the teachings on the physical level—may just be a symbol for a certain energy that becomes available through total surrender or a total opening of the mind. Then the blockages completely disappear, and power radiates forth, so that inner experience unfolds spontaneously.

Today those who are really looking for truth may deeply wonder if there is someone who can give them the true teaching, the true message, the true understanding. Inspired by their own sense of inner truth, they may feel a deep longing for such a guide or friend. But it is not always easy to find such a person, especially in these days of the Kāli Yuga, when human beings seem caught up in confusion and contradiction. It may be that the teacher turns out to have faults, or that someone who makes a connection to a teacher later finds that the 'connection' that seemed so strong and important is really based on his or her own projections.

Perhaps the difficulty comes with the expectations that we have. If we look for the one who is perfect and enlightened—the one who never makes any mistakes—we may find that we are always dissatisfied. But this ideal in any case seems misguided. It ignores the fact that in the end the guru is there to activate something in our own consciousness. Traditionally the true teacher or guru *is* the Buddha, but at the same time, the teacher is also the catalyst, the one who guides and even pushes us to realize our own enlightened nature. It is a complex situation.

Although it is said that the guru is inseparable from the Buddhas of past, present, and future, there are many ways to understand this teaching. As a general principle it seems best not to start with a literal understanding. If you proceed literally, you will expect the teacher to be a certain way, and this expectation will become an obstacle. Instead, let go of expectations. Simply consider the relationship with the teacher as the total situation through which you become enlightened.

The Buddha himself said, "Whoever in the future explains my teaching manifests as my body, my speech, my energy." Seeing in this way creates an opening, and once that opening is there, it is possible that the special quality of the guru—the quality of enlightenment—can blossom right there, within your own consciousness. Then it does not really matter whether the external instrument of transmission is imperfect, or even in some sense broken. You can still receive meaningful knowledge through that instrument.

Another way to say it is that essentially a guru means a true friend. A true friend is someone who can offer guidance, someone who can help a person in trouble to get out of that situation. In that sense, every person and every situation can be your teacher, friend, and guide—even if you must sometimes be guided over very painful ground.

How much and in what ways a teacher becomes available to you will depend very much on how open you are. Investigate these things more closely within your own nature. Once you have really worked on developing awareness within yourself, then the teacher can more readily appear, and can appear in appropriate ways. In fact, everything in your relationship with the teacher will appear appropriate.

Just as the world is two-thirds water, a human being is made up mostly of emotions. Caught up in emotions, we have very little clarity and very little opportunity to know our own nature. But the emotions also express our heartfelt sense that there is something we are missing. Just looking at how emotion dominates our lives, we recognize that we feel a great yearning. We do not know exactly what it is we are searching for, but there is something we need to contact. We need support; we need to be fulfilled. It is just these feelings that need to be opened if we want to understand what the relationship between teacher and student is all about.

When we open the heart completely, this is the same as great love. It is when the heart is not open, or is only partly open, that love manifests as a great yearning. Since that is so, our yearning and our emotions can become a starting point. From there, we can develop more awareness; we can discover who we really are and how our minds work. As emotions subside, love can make itself felt, and the grace or blessing of the guru can flow freely. There is no reason for concern. When such feelings are awakened within us, we will know it directly and unmistakably.

This path toward openness, which finds its natural expression in devotion and surrender, is one that we must travel for ourselves. We cannot rely on friends or lovers; we cannot trust parents; we cannot expect help from society. There is no one 'out there' who can really fulfill us. Externally we may say, "I have my friends and family, I have my work," but internally we are very much alone. Nor is this being alone a sign that something is wrong 'here', so that we need to go 'there'. It is mostly human nature to be alone.

But this loneliness is also a sign that *on our own* we can make a fundamental change. Taking our loneliness as a teaching, we can see that our need for 'something' cannot be satisfied through lesser truths or transient, selfish loves.

This recognition can be the opening we need. Aware of our own nature, aware of the source of our own innermost longing, we can seek out someone we can truly rely on, someone in whom we can take refuge, someone to whom we can completely surrender, without doubt or worry or hesitation. This surrender is not a losing of ourself; perhaps we could say it is a losing of our emotionality, because now it is no longer needed. Now we are at last free to act through our own understanding, our own open heart, our own awakened energy. This is what the guru offers. A mirror of our own highest capacities, he activates our own source of inner knowledge and offers us complete fulfillment.

Original Publication Data

"Foreword," by Tarthang Tulku, drawn from the Prefaces to *Crystal Mirror*, Volumes I, II, and III.

"Introduction," by Tarthang Tulku, revised version of "Studying the Dharma," *Crystal Mirror III*, pp. 112–114.

"The Life of Śākyamuni Buddha," from *Crystal Mirror III*, pp. 21–31.

"Three Paths to Liberation," revised version of "The Three Yanas," *Crystal Mirror I*, pp. 2–4.

"Guru Padmasambhava," from *Crystal Mirror I*, pp. 17–18.

"The Development of Tibetan Buddhism," from *Crystal Mirror I*, pp. 5–16.

"The Marriage of Srong-btsan-sgam-po," from *Gesar Magazine* Vol. VI, No. 4, pp. 20–22; Part II from Vol. VII, No. 1, pp. 27–29.

"rNying-ma Lineage Holders," revised version of "Folio I: The Nyingmapa Lineage," *Crystal Mirror I*, pp. 19–28.

"The Seven Gurus of Tarthang Tulku," revised version of "Folio II: The Gurus of Tarthang Tulku," *Crystal Mirror I,* pp. 45–50.

"Orienting the Mind to the Dharma," by Klong-chen-pa, from *Gesar Magazine,* Vol. VIII, No. 4, pp. 6–8.

"How to Hear the Teachings," by dPal-sprul Rinpoche, from *Gesar Magazine,* Vol. IV, No. 4, pp. 15–18.

"The Teaching of the Essential Point," by Lama Mi-pham, from *Crystal Mirror II,* pp. 40–43.

"The Mark of the Mahāyāna," from "Wishing Prayers," *Gesar Magazine,* Vol. VII, No. 1, pp. 22–23.

"A Ladder to Liberation," from *Gesar Magazine,* Vol. VII, No. 4, pp. 8–9.

"One Flavor," from "Words from Paltrul Rinpoche," *Gesar Magazine,* Vol. VI, No. 3, p. 5.

"The Four Demons," by Ma-gcig Lab-sgron-ma, from "Demons: Routing the Forces of Obstruction," from *Gesar Magazine,* Vol. III, No. 1, pp. 6–9.

"A Look into the Sky-Like Mirror," from *Crystal Mirror III,* pp. 41–45.

"Instructions on Attaining Inner Calm," by Lama Mi-pham, from *Gesar Magazine,* Vol. IV, No. 1, pp. 5–8.

"Mind Is the Root," by Lama Mi-pham, from *Crystal Mirror III,* pp. 3–6.

"Firmly Tie the Mind," from *Crystal Mirror III,* pp. 78–79.

"Prayer to Śākyamuni Buddha," by Lama Mi-pham, from *Gesar Magazine,* Vol. VIII, No. 3, p. 6–7.

"Vajra Guru Mantra," from a gTer-ma of Karma Gling-pa, from *Crystal Mirror II,* pp. 16–39.

"How to Practice the Teachings," by dPal-sprul Rinpoche, from "Taking the Medicine of the Teacher," *Gesar Magazine,* Vol. VII, No. 3, pp. 15–18.

"One Moon," by dPal-sprul Rinpoche, from *Gesar Magazine,* Vol. VIII, No. 2, p. 4.

"dPal-sprul Rinpoche's Counsels," from *Crystal Mirror I,* pp. 39–41.

"Ritual Practice: Entering the Mandala," revised version of "Entering the Mandala," from *Crystal Mirror II,* pp. 60–66.

"An Interview with Tarthang Tulku," from *Crystal Mirror II,* pp. 9–16.

"On Thoughts," from *Crystal Mirror III,* pp. 7–20.

"Transmuting Energies through Breath," from *Crystal Mirror III,* pp. 46–48.

"Waking Up to Infinite Possibilities," by Tarthang Tulku, from *Gesar Magazine,* Vol. V, No. 1, pp. 2–6.

"The Nature of Laziness," by Tarthang Tulku, from "Vigor," *Crystal Mirror I,* pp. 74–75.

"The Prize of True Understanding," by Tarthang Tulku, revised version of "Excerpt from a Lecture," *Crystal Mirror I,* pp. 77–78.

"Situational Patterning," by Steven D. Goodman, from *Crystal Mirror III,* pp. 93–101.

"How to Meditate," by Tarthang Tulku, from *Gesar Magazine,* Vol. V, No. 1, pp. 4–6.

"Analyzing the Judging Mind," by Tarthang Tulku, revised version of "Judgment," *Crystal Mirror II,* pp. 52–57.

"Mind and Feelings," by Tarthang Tulku, from *Crystal Mirror III,* pp. 76–79.

"The Self-Image," by Tarthang Tulku, from *Crystal Mirror III,* pp. 32–40.

"Friend, Teacher, and Guru," by Tarthang Tulku, from *Gesar Magazine,* Vol. III, No. 4, pp. 2–7.

Index

ༀ་ དབལ་ ཆེན་ མགོན་པོ་ ཕྱག་ བཞི་ པ །

Tarthang Tulku

About Tarthang Tulku: A Note from the Staff of Dharma Publishing

The general editor for the *Crystal Mirror Series* is Tarthang Tulku, an accomplished Tibetan lama who has made his home in the United States for the past twenty-three years. Since his arrival in India in 1959, Rinpoche has worked with complete dedication for the transmission of the Dharma. As his students, we have learned to find inspiration in his tireless devotion and profound respect for the Dharma.

For seven years while he was living in India, Rinpoche taught at Sanskrit University in Varanasi, establishing an international reputation as a scholar. During this time he founded Dharma Mudranalaya and began publishing texts from the Tibetan Buddhist tradition. He has continued this work in America for over twenty years. Today books by Dharma Publishing, including a number of translations of important Buddhist texts, have been adopted for use in more than five hundred colleges and universities throughout the world.

In addition to his work as a scholar and publisher, Rinpoche has been active as an author and educator. He has written nine books presenting teachings for the modern world, produced two translations, and served as editor of the Nyingma Edition of the Tibetan Buddhist Canon, the Research Catalogue of the Nyingma Edition, and the Guide to the Nyingma Edition. He is founder and president of the Nyingma Institute in Berkeley and its affiliated centers, where several thousand students have come in contact with the Dharma.

In the midst of all these activities, Rinpoche has also found time to serve in the traditional role of teacher for a growing community of Western students. Always willing to experiment, he has established a form of practice for his students in which their work on behalf of the Dharma becomes a path to realization. Many of his students do not have frequent direct contact with Rinpoche, but through the institutions he has established, they are able to grow in wisdom and understanding, while developing practical skills that enable them to make their way in the world. Above all, Rinpoche has devoted much of his energy to the creation of Odiyan, a country center that he hopes will one day change the basis for Dharma practice in the West.

Because of the incredible range of activities in which Rinpoche engages during a single day, it has not been possible for him to verify the accuracy of every element of the books we have produced under his direction. As a result, there may be mistakes in some of the material presented here, for which we take full responsibility. We only hope that on balance we have been successful in transmitting some elements of the Dharma tradition.

Those of us who have had the opportunity to work under Rinpoche in the production of Dharma Publishing books are deeply grateful for the example he has set us. His dedication and reliable knowledge, his steady, untiring efforts, his competence, and his caring allow us to direct our energy with complete confidence that despite our own imperfections, our work can be of benefit to others.